THE
GPO

200 YEARS OF HISTORY

THE
GPO

200 YEARS OF HISTORY

STEPHEN FERGUSON

MERCIER PRESS
Irish Publisher – Irish Story

MERCIER PRESS

Cork

www.mercierpress.ie

© Stephen Ferguson, 2014

ISBN: 978 1 78117 277 3

10 9 8 7 6 5 4 3 2 1

A CIP record for this title is available from the British Library

Printed and bound in the EU

CONTENTS

T. C. Thompson's (c. 1780–1857) portrait of Francis Johnston (1760–1829), showing him against a backdrop of the GPO, captures a certain melancholy in the architect's temperament.
(© National Museums Northern Ireland, Ulster Museum Collection)

ACKNOWLEDGEMENTS

I am grateful to those in various institutions, both public and private, who have helped me with my research and kindly allowed me to reproduce material in their care. I had particular assistance from Ciara Baker, John Bowman, Paddy Clarke, Noel Collins, David Davison, Julian Deale, Lydia Ferguson, Bob Fitzsimons, Aideen Ireland, Carla Killeen, Caroline Lemka, John Lennon, Simon Lincoln, David MacDonnell, Dieter Michelson, Héloise Mitchell, Vicky Parkinson, Colum O'Riordan, the Earl and Countess of Rosse, Glenn Thomson and Brian Warren. I also appreciate the support of Post Office colleagues, past and present, who share my interest in and fondness for the GPO.

Unless otherwise indicated, all images form part of the GPO's Museum and Archive collections and are reproduced courtesy of An Post.

8

Street

Street

Street

G. Abby Street

Walk

Batchelors

Quay

RIVER

As tons

Q

Q

Fleet Street

College

30

29

28

34

College Green

27

Dames Str

32

31

Chequer

Georges Lane

Chea ter La.

n Street

ndon Street

fton Str

Naſs

The Post Office
in Ireland

❧ ❧

There came one morning a letter with the Roman post-mark, and addressed, 'à Monsieur le Vicompte de Kilgobbin, à son Château de Kilgobbin, en Irlande'. To the honour of the officials in the Irish post-office, it was forwarded to Kilgobbin with the words, 'Try Mathew Kearney, Esq.', in the corner.

Charles Lever, *Lord Kilgobbin*

❧ ❧

Charles Lever's novels are no longer widely read, but behind the stage Irishness that appealed to his largely English readership, there are many insights into social and political life in nineteenth-century Ireland. Occasional postal references punctuate his stories and it is perhaps fitting that the story of the GPO should begin with a quotation from one of Lever's novels, because his father, James, was a Dublin builder and was reputed to have worked with Francis Johnston on the construction of the General Post Office. The Post Office, of course, predates the GPO and is one of the oldest institutions of the state. Its origins lie in the political and military turmoil of the sixteenth and seventeenth centuries, when a system of communication became vital to English policy in Ireland. Communication between London and Dublin was a slow and hazardous affair: boats were small, the sea passage was rough and the financial arrangements between the government and the boat owners were such that captains would often sail only when additional cargo and passengers made it worth their while.

James Gillray's caricature of 1805, with its broken-down coach, ramshackle inn and brutal inhabitants, must have done little for the tourist industry of the time. In fact the Post Office's regular mail-coach network, helped by investment in road building, generally offered the traveller a less frightening experience.

Within Ireland, while mounted messengers, or 'intelligencers' as they were sometimes called, were used by the King and great noblemen for the delivery of letters, no formal arrangement for the delivery of mail existed until the establishment in the 1640s by Evan Vaughan, the postmaster in Dublin, of a staging system along the three main roads out of Dublin: south to Cork and Limerick, west to Galway and Sligo and north to Belfast and Londonderry. Post boys, on foot or on horseback, set out twice a week carrying official and commercial letters. It was Oliver Cromwell, remembered for his terrible tyranny in Ireland, who outlawed private postal services in 1657 and set up a state monopoly that remains, in a much reduced form, even today.

More peaceful conditions in the eighteenth century allowed the Post Office in Ireland to expand. Local postmasters were appointed by the state, surveyors were charged with carrying out checks on the post boys, the postal network was extended and the first mail-coaches were

OPPOSITE: *In contrast to Gillray, Hugh Thomson, the Coleraine-born artist and illustrator, provides an idealised view of a world in which post boys and postilions follow their fathers into a noble profession. A particular GPO connection exists in that Thomson illustrated a book for A. H. Norway, Post Office secretary at the time of the 1916 Rising.*

The loves and jealousies of Two Jolly Postboys.

By Hugh Thomson.

Tom and Jerry were two jolly postboys who had lived in
great friendship from boyhood. Their fathers had been postboys before them, until, growing too stout for the profession,
they had handed their traditions on to our heroes, giving
each much good advice and a pair of top boots. In the
village where they were born and brought up there also lived
pretty Polly Flinders, and Tom and Jerry when at school had
each cast looks of favour upon her. But when each discovered
that the other received surreptitious presents of stickjaw and
lollipops from her, their youthful friendship sustained a severe
shock, and betaking themselves to the retirement of a neighbouring
field, they divested themselves of their jackets, and, falling to, a
battle like knights of yore for the smiles of their Queen
Beauty. Jerry, who had previously eaten more stickjaw than
was consistent with the proper gladiatorial training, suffered
severely during the first part of the encounter; but as the fight
waxed hot his natural impetuosity overcame this drawback, un-

introduced in 1789. Certain remote areas, though well populated, remained difficult to reach, and easy communication with the capital was by no means assured. Cahirciveen, in County Kerry, for instance, was 160 Irish miles from Dublin and occasionally received Dublin correspondence via New York, with letters and newspapers having twice traversed the Atlantic Ocean![1] For the majority of Irish people, however, the way the mails were sent was a matter of small concern, for postal charges were high and effectively put the service beyond their reach.

A 'Penny Post' service, distinct from the general post, was started in Dublin in 1773 and this provided a very efficient and much cheaper way of corresponding within city and suburban limits. One contemporary account records that 'the letters are delivered four times a day with such celerity and exactness, that two persons living at opposite extremities of the city may write four letters and receive three answers every day'.[2] This system of penny and later twopenny posts was gradually extended to provincial towns, but it was Rowland Hill's successful campaign for standardised penny postage throughout Britain and Ireland that in 1840 opened up the great benefits of the Post Office to ordinary people. Following legislative independence in 1782, an independent Irish Post Office was set up in 1784. It lasted until 1831, when concerns over financial management prompted a return of authority to the postmaster general in London.

The Victorian era saw the development of the modern Post Office in Ireland. Railways won Post Office contracts for the carriage of mail, putting an end to the mail-coach system and the 'Bian' long cars introduced by that enterprising and popular immigrant, Charles Bianconi. Competition for lucrative mail contracts on the Dublin to Holyhead sea route meant that for many years the world's fastest steamships were to be found on the Irish Sea. Post to rural areas was

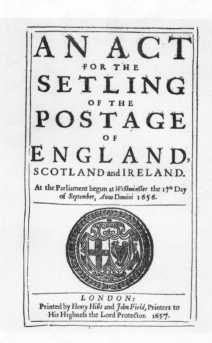

Oliver Cromwell recognised the strategic importance of communications, and this Act of Parliament, through the creation of a monopoly, firmly established state control of the business in Britain and Ireland.

---

1. The Irish mile, at 2,240 yds, was equal to 1.27 statute or English miles. Although the unit was legally abolished in 1824, it continued to be used by the Post Office for some years and survived in parts of rural Ireland until the end of the century.

2. McGregor, J. J., *New Picture of Dublin* (Archer, Dublin, 1821), p. 80.

The mail-coach conveyed passengers as well as mail. This illustration shows a bustling scene as emigrants prepare to leave Cahirciveen, in County Kerry.

greatly extended, not least due to the efforts of the novelist Anthony Trollope, who spent several years working for the Post Office in Ireland. To him, too, must go the credit for the introduction of that most useful of Post Office improvements, the pillar box.

Gradually the Post Office assumed a role as the principal, and generally benign, agent of government throughout the country. The Post Office Savings Bank was established in 1861, and in 1909 old-age pensions were first paid through the Post Office. With its services covering so many aspects of everyday life – from mails and banking to telegraphs and telephones – the Post Office was the greatest department of the state.

Following Irish independence in 1922, Post Office functions were transferred to the new Department of Posts and Telegraphs, which faced considerable difficulties in its early years. Deliveries in rural areas were gradually extended, motorised transport was introduced and the telephone network was expanded. Radio broadcasting, which had had a small office in Little Denmark Street, on the site where the ILAC shopping centre stands today, moved into the GPO, where studios had been provided on the third and fourth floors of the Henry Street wing of the building. From modest beginnings Radio Éireann grew in importance and the presence of various personalities brought some colour and glamour to the GPO. When the station moved

A public notice for 1792, issued under the signature of John Lees, Post Office secretary, detailing the scheduled dispatch times for English mails.

out to Donnybrook in 1973, the place lost a bit of its excitement. In 1984 the postal functions of the department were transferred to a new state company, An Post, which was created to manage the postal business on a more commercial basis. Technological advances and automated processing have transformed operations since then and the postal market itself has changed radically, but the Post Office's long tradition of useful service to the state and its citizens remains.

The Post Office, of course, was a very much smaller operation in the seventeenth and eighteenth centuries and there was nothing in those days quite like the General Post Office as we know it today. Since it existed primarily as part of the government's administration of the country, it is not surprising to find it situated quite close to the seat of power in Dublin Castle. Records for this period are scant but the shift in the location of the Post Office in Dublin can be seen in the maps and street directories that survive. As the city centre has gradually moved east over the last 300 years, so has the city's Post Office – from High Street in 1668 to Fishamble Street in 1689 to Sycamore Alley in 1709 and then in 1755 to Bardin's Chocolate House on the site now occupied by the Central Bank. In those early days the Post

Bianconi spotted the opportunity to set up a cheap passenger service that offered transport on the many routes not served by mail-coaches. His Post Office contracts for conveying the mails helped to finance the passenger business.

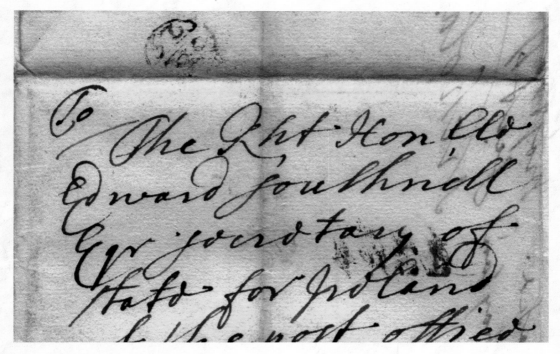

This letter from 1717 is for Edward Southwell, who succeeded his father as secretary of state
for Ireland, and is addressed simply to the recipient 'at the post office Dublin'.

Office drew its business mainly from a small group of people associated with the commercial and political interests of the city. Many of these men met in a famous coffee house of the time, Dick's Coffee-house, the proprietor of which was Richard Pue, who, besides making 'the best coffee in Dublin', published one of the earliest Irish newspapers, *Pue's Occurrences*. Dick's Coffee-house was situated in Skinner's Row (near where Jury's Inn Christchurch stands today) not far from the GPO in Sycamore Alley, and Tom Geraghty, who worked in Dick's, wrote in 1740 a few interesting lines to his customers, the 'citizens, gentlemen, lawyers and squires' who 'live upon politicks, coffee and news':

> Poor Tom daily serves you and carries your letters
> Unto the Post-office, wherefore you stand debtors;
> For three times a week he must carry a pack
> Well cramm'd with epistles, on shoulder and back,
> He snuffs all your candles, and nothing denies you
> With pen, ink and wafers, he, gratis, supplies you.[3]

---

3. Gilbert, J. T., *A History of the City of Dublin* (McGlashan and Gill, Dublin, 1859), p. 175.

Radio — for many just the 'wireless' — was broadcast from the GPO and helped, by means of news, sport and music, to forge a sense of national identity in the young Irish state.

Dick's Coffee-house had closed by the time of Irish legislative independence in 1782, but Dublin had grown in size and confidence and the heart of the city was now centred on College Green. Here learning and legislation met, with Trinity College at the centre and the Parliament House (now the Bank of Ireland) on the north side of the Green. Keeping an eye on them both was the General Post Office, which had moved from its old Fownes' Court premises in 1783. The building was situated on the south side, slightly raised from the pavement and ideally positioned for anyone who wanted to observe the comings and goings of Irish parliamentarians and seek, perhaps, a quick word or arrange a meeting on a matter of importance. It was on the steps of the Post Office, indeed, that not long after legislative union with Great Britain, Curran, the famous barrister, was approached by one of those who had been induced to vote for the abolition of the Irish Parliament. Sorrowfully shaking his head, he observed, 'How shocking our old Parliament-house looks, Curran!' Well versed in his Shakespeare, the witty and erudite lawyer quickly replied, 'True, my Lord; it is usual for murderers to be afraid of ghosts'.

The GPO in College Green was housed in a substantial four-storey building on the site now occupied by the Abercrombie & Fitch shop. An engraving from 1787 shows the plain Georgian block that housed the city's Post Office. It was not only the meeting point for those who wished to send or receive letters but also the first place where English and foreign news might be sought.

OPPOSITE: *The government was for many years keen to encourage saving through the Post Office, and posters like this brought the advantages of regular, planned saving to the attention of the public.*

OVERLEAF: *A detail from a 1770 map of Dublin which shows the location (marked at No. 29) of the GPO at Fownes' Court, a site now occupied by the Central Bank.* (Author's Collection)

Dreaming won't do it —

SAVINGS CERTIFICATES

Will

8

Street

G. Abby Street

Walk

Street

Street

Batchelors

Quay

R I V E R

Astons

Fleet Street

30

29

Co

28

34

College Gr

Dames

Str

32

Chequer

31

Lane

ter La.

Street

Street

Str

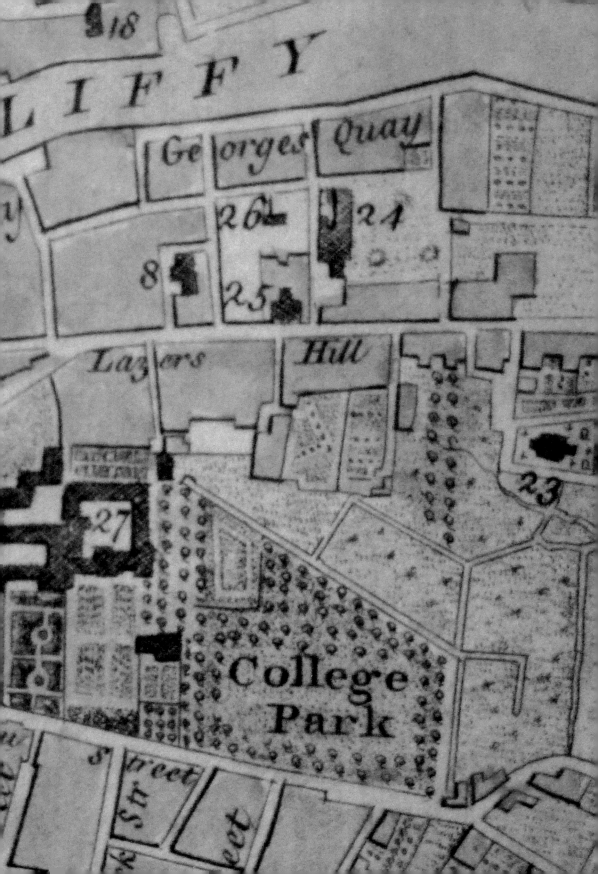

Sir John Carr, the observant if rather pedantic Englishman who published his account of a visit to Ireland in 1805, complained that the Post Office was the place 'where the ear is annoyed with newsmen, crying out, "Two packets, two packets": meaning that the news, which they hold in their hands, contain [*sic*] the intelligence brought by that number of packets last arrived from England.'[4] The 1787 engraving also shows another building beside the Post Office, set back slightly from the street. This was the house of the Post Office secretary or chief executive of the day and the accommodation was provided with the job.

On the establishment of an independent Irish Post Office in 1784, the College Green premises had been transferred from the postmaster general of Great Britain to the postmaster general of Ireland, but the building was not well adapted to Post Office needs and 'from the great Increase of Business of the said General Post Office in *Dublin*, the said Premises are now insufficient for the Purposes of the said Establishment'.[5] The building's fabric was indeed in a very poor state, with ceilings close to collapse and accommodation generally unsuitable for business. Consideration was consequently given to extending the premises into adjoining property in Suffolk Street, occupied by the Incorporated Law Society, and an act of parliament 'to enable his Majesty's Postmaster General of *Ireland* to purchase Premises for the enlargement of the General Post Office in the City of *Dublin*' was duly passed in May 1807. Very little progress, however, was made over the next couple of years except that, in the course of legal discussion on extending the premises into neighbouring

> General Post-Office Dublin, Oct. 14. 1742.
>
> WHereas divers Persons, thro' Ignorance or Carelesness frequently put Letters into the General Post-Office, d Let ther Post Offices in the Country, directed on board of Ships, to foreign Parts, and to Scotland, without paying at the same time the Postage, as ought to be done; And whereas Letters and Packets are often put into the said Offices with Money and Rings inclosed, and in Fraud o his Majesty's Revenue, divers Persons presume to send Letters with False and COUNTERFEIT FRANKS.
> This is to acquaint the Publick, that no Letters under any of the Circumstances aforesaid have any right by Law to be forwarded,
> Note, That Letters going out of Ireland (except to France, Holland and Flanders) have by the ancient Usage of the Post-Office, paid the Postage to London, as well as the foreign Postage, and are required by the Act of Parliament so to do, at the Office in Ireland, where the same are first put in.
> Note also, that Letters directed to France, Holland and Flanders, are only to pay the Postage to London, and those directed to Scotland, the Sea-Postage between Donaghadee and Port-Patrick, which must be paid at the Office, where the same first are put in.
> By Order of Sir Marmaduke Wyvill, Bart.
> EDWARD MARTIN.

This GPO notice, published in Pue's Occurrences *in 1742, highlights the challenges the Post Office faced to protect its revenue, with both ignorance and fraud accounting for significant financial loss and administrative inconvenience.*

4.   Carr, J., *The Stranger in Ireland* (Richard Philips, London, 1806), p. 84.

5.   48 Geo. III, c. 48, An Post archives.

buildings, it was discovered that the Post Office, despite the earlier conveyance from the British postmaster general, did not have clear title to its existing premises. This necessitated the passing of an amending act authorising the postmaster general to purchase 'the Ground and Premises whereon the said Post Office has been erected and now stands'.[6] By the spring of 1813, the year after the adjoining tenements had eventually been purchased, the potential of an alternative site in Sackville Street was being considered in some quarters, while the Wide Streets Commissioners were strongly advocating the merits of constructing a GPO on the site of the old Custom House on Essex Quay. Their argument highlighted the savings to be made by reusing some of the Custom House materials in the new Post Office, a notion that Francis Johnston of the Board of Works dismissed as a false economy. His views had been sought on the proposals which had advanced to the degree that there existed both a design proposal, by a Mr Greves, for a new

This drawing from the Gentleman's Magazine *of 1787 shows the extent of the College Green GPO, with, on the left of the picture, the house that was used to accommodate the Post Office secretary.*

6. 49 Geo. III, c. 70, An Post archives.

ANNO QUADRAGESIMO OCTAVO

GEORGII III. REGIS.

‡‡

C A P. XLVIII.

An Act to enable His Majesty's Postmaster General of *Ireland* to purchase Premises for the Enlargement of the General Post Office in the City of Dublin. [27th May 1807.]

WHEREAS by an Act passed in the Parliament of *Ireland*, in the Twenty-third and Twenty-fourth Years of the Reign of His present Majesty, for establishing a Post Office in that Kingdom, it was enacted, that as soon as conveniently might be after the passing of said Act, there should be a General Letter Office and Post Office established in some convenient Place within the City of *Dublin*, with Sub-offices throughout *Ireland*, from whence all Letters and Packets whatsoever to or from Places within *Ireland* or beyond Seas, might with Speed and Expedition be sent, received, and dispatched: And whereas by an Act, passed by the Parliament of *Great Britain* in the Twenty-fourth Year of the Reign of His present Majesty, intituled, *An Act for establishing certain Regulations concerning the Postage and Conveyance of Letters and Packets by the Post, between Great Britain and Ireland*, His Majesty's Post Master General of *Great Britain* was authorized and empowered to grant and convey to His Majesty's Postmaster General of *Ireland*, certain Buildings erected in *Dublin* and known by the Name of *The General Post Office in Ireland*: And whereas the said Premises were accordingly duly conveyed by His Majesty's Postmaster General of *Great Britain* to His Majesty's Postmaster General of *Ireland*: And whereas from the great Increase of Business of the said General Post Office in *Dublin*, the said Premises are now insufficient for the Purposes of the said Establishment, and it is necessary and expedient to make considerable Additions thereto; be it therefore enacted by the King's most Excellent Majesty, by and with the Advice and Consent of the Lords Spiritual and Temporal, and Commons, in this present Parliament assembled, and by the Authority of the same,

This 1807 Act of Parliament is one of several that dealt with the extension or relocation of the GPO in the early nineteenth century.

GPO on the expanded College Green/Suffolk Street site and another, by a Mr Chisney, for the erection of a Post Office in Sackville Street. In the end, the Lord Lieutenant ended the wrangling by taking the decision himself. He rejected extension in favour of entirely new premises for the GPO, which would bid farewell, after a long sojourn there, to the south side and move across the River Liffey to take up residence in the increasingly fashionable Sackville Street area of the city.

In May 1814 an act was passed giving the postmaster general of Ireland power to sell the old College Green GPO and to purchase instead buildings and land 'in order … that a new and more convenient Post Office may be made, erected, and built'.[7] The College Green Post Office was bought for £11,000 by an enterprising businessman who converted it into what must have been the city's earliest shopping centre, the Royal Arcade, where top-quality items were sold to the discerning Dublin shopper. The Arcade was designed by Francis Johnston, who was also to be the architect of the new GPO across the river. It retained a postal connection

A pair of candle sticks from the College Green GPO.

7.   54 Geo. III, c. 63, An Post archives.

Following the sale of the GPO in College Green, the premises were bought by the businessman George Homes and converted into a two-storey shopping arcade which linked College Green with Suffolk Street. (Author's Collection)

as it was home to a receiving house, or sub-post office, and it flourished until it was completely destroyed by a fire in 1837. The commercial importance of College Green ensured that a GPO branch post office survived there, just a few doors down from the old GPO site, until the building on the corner of Church Lane was acquired by the Ulster Bank in the early 1970s.

Francis Johnston
and the new
GPO

☙ ❧

Commodious, well arranged ... and highly ornamental to the city.

J. N. Brewer on the GPO

☙ ❧

The upper end of Sackville Street, complete with a tree-lined mall, had been elegantly designed by one of Dublin's greatest property developers, Luke Gardiner, in the mid-eighteenth century, but what is now Lower O'Connell Street did not exist at the time, and maps of the period show that there was no straight street line between the river and Parnell Square as there is now. The area was ready for the sort of urban redevelopment favoured by the Wide Streets Commissioners and the site on which the GPO now stands had been examined as a possible location for the city's Roman Catholic cathedral. A degree of religious intolerance, however, was still evident in Dublin and it was felt that a less prominent position, fronting onto Marlborough Street, might cause less controversy. The site was occupied by a number of houses that had been used as a temporary military barracks, but the construction had been poor and the buildings 'so shaken by their numerous inmates', as G. N. Wright records, that they collapsed, the soldiers and their families barely having time to escape.[1] The plot was secured for the Post Office

---

1. Wright, G. N., *An Historical Guide to the City of Dublin* (Four Courts Press/Irish Academic Press, Dublin, 1980, reprint of 1825 ed.) p. 166.

The detail above from a 1770 map of Dublin shows a truncated Sackville Street, Gardiner's Mall (as seen in the street view below) and the area that would be developed to extend the street towards the River Liffey and on which the new GPO would be built. (Map: Author's Collection)

and the opportunity arose to create an uninterrupted view stretching from the D'Olier and Westmoreland Street apex on the south side of the Liffey, across the new Carlisle Bridge and up Sackville Street to the Rotunda. At the time a few people contended that the site was too far removed from the city centre, but this was a temporary inconvenience and was in great measure counterbalanced by the extent of the building space provided by the unusual width of Sackville Street. One English traveller and author, commenting on the GPO, found 'The whole edifice ... honourable to the present state of architectural talent in this country' and 'the necessity for so spacious a pile ... a grateful proof of an increasing interchange that cannot fail to prove of the highest national advantage'.[2]

In considering the situation and architecture of the GPO, it would be easy now to overlook the importance of Nelson's Pillar, the massive Doric column that was built in 1808 and which dominated O'Connell Street until its untimely destruction in 1966. The great architectural historian of Dublin, Maurice Craig, saw the two structures as reciprocal, with the capacity 'to redeem O'Connell Street, potentially so beautiful, from a squalid disorder almost equal to parts of London'.[3] In contrast to the rather inhuman and useless modernity of the Spire ('a stainless-steel needle ... with clearly visible joints and a nasty mirror-patterned base'), which is so much at odds with the Post Office, the Pillar and the GPO were complementary structures and provided a symmetry, balance and harmony of style that added to the grandeur of a street that regularly impressed visitors to the city.[4] Erected in honour of Admiral Nelson, the hero of Trafalgar, the Duke of Richmond laid the foundation stone in February 1808 and the column was finished in time for a formal opening ceremony on 21 October 1809, the anniversary of that famous battle. The Pillar was periodically the subject of political controversy, but by the time republican sympathisers blew it up, it had won a place of affection in the hearts of most Dubliners because, standing 134 ft high, it provided not only an excellent view of the capital and its surroundings but also a readily identifiable assembly point for the city's trams and buses. It was designed by William Wilkins, who had been selected following a public competition, and paid for – rather reluctantly it has to be said – by voluntary subscription, one of the contributors being Sir John Lees of the GPO. The original design was somewhat extravagant and required modification, and in this Francis Johnston 'afforded the necessary assistance with his acknowledged ability, which, notwithstanding his various and important avocations, he did with the utmost cheerfulness'.[5]

Johnston has perhaps been rather neglected over the years and he was certainly unlucky in that several of his buildings fell victim to modification, neglect or destruction, not least the

---

2. Brewer, J. N., *The Beauties of Ireland* (Sherwood, Jones, London, 1825), p. 89.

3. Craig, M., *Dublin 1660–1860* (Cresset Press, London, 1952), p. 287.

4. Casey, C., *Dublin* (Yale University Press, New Haven, 2005), p. 220.

5. National Library of Ireland (NLI) Ms. 20,845: *Nelson's Pillar: A Description of the Pillar with a List of Subscribers*.

PREVIOUS PAGES AND ABOVE: *George Petrie's oblique view of Nelson's Pillar and the GPO portico, a view mirrored in a photograph taken nearly a century and a half later, highlights the compositional harmony that existed between the two structures* (engraving: Author's Collection, photograph courtesy of Davison & Associates). *This sense of balance and proportion was not reproduced when the Spire was completed in 2003* (Spire photograph courtesy of Catalyst DNA).

GPO and the Royal Hibernian Academy, both of which suffered in 1916. Yet enough remains of his work on buildings like St George's church in Dublin, Townley Hall in County Louth and Charleville Forest in County Offaly, as well as the GPO façade, to show that he was an architect of considerable distinction, at home in both the neoclassical and the Gothic traditions. That he regarded the GPO as his greatest achievement may be inferred perhaps from T. C. Thompson's painting in the Ulster Museum, which portrays him against the backdrop of the Post Office.

By birth Johnston was a County Armagh man, whose family had Scottish antecedents and a long pedigree in building work, a William Johnston having come to Ireland from Scotland to make repairs to buildings damaged in the rebellion of 1641. It is a curious historical irony that the repairs he undertook after one Irish rebellion should be counterbalanced by the destruction wrought on his descendant's work in the course of another. Francis' father, another William, was also a builder and part-time architect and three of his four sons followed him into the profession.

It was Francis, however, who was destined to achieve recognition as an Irish architect of enduring reputation. He was born in 1760 and came to the notice of the Archbishop of Armagh, Richard Robinson, whose patronage and taste was responsible for much of the architectural

Built in 1799, Townley Hall's restrained dignity displays, within the domestic sphere, Johnston's mastery of the classical idiom (Townley Hall: courtesy of MVK Architects). *In the ecclesiastical field, the spire of St George's in Dublin is beautifully executed while his work on the Chapel Royal in Dublin Castle, of which the interior with the organ is shown here, demonstrates a commensurate capacity to work within a Gothic framework.* (Author's Collection)

elegance still to be found in that city. Robinson had employed Thomas Cooley, responsible for the Royal Exchange (now City Hall) in Dublin, as his architect and he sent the young Johnston to work for him. Cooley employed him to supervise the construction of the Linen Hall, where he would have gained practical experience of overseeing the day-to-day work of builders. His eye for detail and appreciation of the painstaking nature of fine craftsmanship, in wood carving for instance, may be seen in his design for the wine cooler on display in Number Twenty-Nine, the Georgian House Museum, on Fitzwilliam Street Lower. Johnston also spent some time in the office of Samuel Sproul, a busy if uninspiring architect, who undertook work for the Wide Streets Commissioners, and his experience of dealing with its large-scale urban remodelling plans would have stood him in good stead later on when the opportunity arose to build the GPO as part of a redesigned Sackville Street.

When Cooley died in 1784, Johnston succeeded him as the primate's architect and was employed on a number of local schemes. Robinson had asked Cooley to build a new tower, somewhat similar to that of Magdalen College, Oxford, on the cathedral. As the tower soared skywards, some of the more timid churchgoers feared it would collapse on them and they refused to attend services in the cathedral. The archbishop had to stop the work before his entire congregation disappeared. One of Johnston's first jobs was to raise, on the existing foundations, the height of the tower and spire without causing similar anxiety. This was successfully achieved and he also completed the primate's chapel, built by Cooley, creating a delightful interior space. Armagh Observatory is Johnston's creation and he carried out work on both the Roman Catholic and Church of Ireland churches in Drogheda, where he lived for a time before moving to Dublin in 1793.

In 1790 Johnston married Anne Barnes, an Armagh native whose sister was married to his brother Richard. Martin Cregan's picture of Johnston and his wife in the company of his nephews radiates intimacy and a cosy domestic contentment.

A short tour of England in 1796 broadened Johnston's architectural awareness and general artistic outlook. He kept a diary of his trip and his entries show a mind that was not only quick to appreciate and learn from the skills of other craftsmen – whether it was the builders of late medieval houses in Tewkesbury or the architect of St Paul's Cathedral – but was also endowed with a worldly shrewdness that made him a successful businessman. His admiration, for instance, for much of the fine building he saw in Bath is tempered by the

OPPOSITE: *'Francis Johnston, his Wife and Two Nephews' (c. 1827) by Martin Cregan (1788–1870). This is a happy domestic scene, showing Johnston relaxing with his wife, Anne, and two nephews, Andrew and Robert. Signs of his professional and artistic interests are casually juxtaposed with the shuttlecock and racquet on the floor by the dog.* (© National Museums Northern Ireland, Ulster Museum Collection)

St George's, Hardwicke Place — its white stone set off against an ominous sky — was of more than architectural interest to Johnston. It was his local church and he left money for the bells to be rung on certain special occasions. (Courtesy of Davison & Associates)

remark that it was 'a large good town full of fashionable people with amusements of every kind to coax the money out of their pockets'.[6]

Successful work for various private gentlemen brought Johnston's name before a wealthy and influential group of patrons. Work for Blaney Balfour on Townley Hall, for Colonel Conyngham on Slane Castle, for the Earl of Fingall at Killeen Castle and at Charleville Forest for the Earl of Charleville shows that he was able to draw on a distinguished list of private clients. Townley Hall, designed by Johnston in 1794, is an important work that gives clear indications of the influences, temperament and style of the man who would be architect of the GPO some twenty years later. The plain austerity of the exterior and the use of Greek Doric columns betray the influence of James Wyatt, who had built Castle Coole, for which Francis' brother Richard had also submitted

6.   NLI Ms. 2722: *Diary of Francis Johnston Architect, 25th March to 24th April 1796.*

designs. Attention to detail and a capacity for interior decoration and design work are also evident in the construction of Townley Hall. The Greek key pattern makes an appearance in the entrance hall and would emerge again over the years in buildings like St George's church and, of course, the GPO. If Townley Hall sets out the qualities of the young architect, acknowledging the influence of a master but searching for his own style, St George's in Hardwicke Place marks, at least in his ecclesiastical work, the high point of an assured and accomplished artist. No longer in use as a church, the beautiful interior – bright, spacious and, unusually, wider than it is long – is not easily appreciated today, but the wonderful steeple, which Johnston modelled on Gibbs' St Martin in the Fields in London and which rises to 200 ft, is an inspiring Dublin landmark, 'lovely in all lights but lovelier than anything in Dublin when', as one authority aptly expressed it, 'its white stone is seen in a harsh white light against the background of a threatening northern sky'.[7] St George's brought out the best in Johnston. He had a fine spacious site on which to work, and as a local resident – it would become the church he would attend and he would be buried in its graveyard – he also had a particular incentive to create something of special beauty.

His work throughout the country on private commissions, both ecclesiastical and domestic, earned him a reputation that did not escape the notice of the public officials responsible for civic architecture. *Wilson's Dublin Directory* of 1805 lists him simply, along with the assorted shoemakers, tailors and fruiterers of the Merchants and Traders section of the book, as Francis Johnston, architect, 6 Eccles Street, but the year after, following his appointment as successor to Robert Woodgate as architect and inspector of civil buildings, his name was also to be found in Stewart's *Almanack* under the Board of Works listing.[8] This 1805 appointment was an acknowledgement of his high public standing and gave him the opportunity to move beyond churches and private houses to work on public buildings. He had done some fine work on the modifications required by the Bank of Ireland to convert the College Green building from the seat of the Irish Parliament to commercial use, but the particular challenges faced in the design of premises to be used as prisons, lunatic asylums or as a General Post Office were new to him.

OVERLEAF: *A fine early view (1820), drawn by G. H. Jones and engraved by Robert Havell, of Johnston's GPO and the bustling surroundings of Sackville Street. On the left is the Cork mail-coach, with a guard about to throw down a bag to the waiting man, while boys gather round a street vendor on the right.*

---

7. For an assessment of Johnston and his work see Dr Edward McParland's article in the *Quarterly Bulletin of the Irish Georgian Society* (1969) vol. 12, nos. 3 and 4.

8. From the directory entry, it seems that his elder brother, Richard, also an architect, lived in the same street at No. 24. A tangential GPO connection may also be claimed for Richard Johnston. In 1784 he designed the Assembly Room, now in use as the Gate Theatre's auditorium, and the pump room of the Rotunda complex, where the Post Office established an emergency sorting office in 1916.

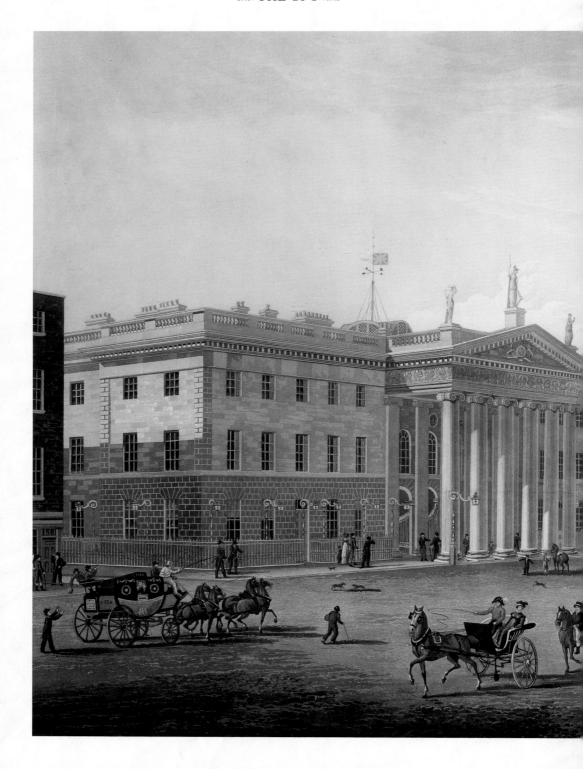

To each building he brought an integrity of approach that sought to blend his stark architectural simplicity with the practical requirements of its function. He was required to develop a new perspective, one that directed his thoughts away from the modification of noble seats and the creation of castellated houses for the gentry to practical consideration of what constituted suitable housing for prisoners and psychiatric patients. This type of work for the Board of Works – large-scale institutional building – as seen in his designs for the Richmond Penitentiary and the Armagh Lunatic Asylum, necessarily obliged him to concentrate on the harsher aspects of life and humanity. It is greatly to his credit that he approached his work with a genuine desire to understand the nature and use of the buildings he was being asked to design and the particular needs of those who would live there.

The Richmond Penitentiary, for instance, on which Johnston began to work in 1810, reflects a keen and sympathetic appreciation of the aims of prison reformers who focused on prison accommodation and conditions as critical elements in the moral reform of prisoners. The space was carefully planned to provide individual cells, exercise yards, chapels, an infirmary and even a shop where goods manufactured by the prisoners could be sold to the public. Completed some five years before a similar building was opened in London, the ingenuity and innovation of Johnston's plans are notable and, while he has sometimes been criticised for what might be seen as the cold severity of his exteriors, he deserves particular recognition for what Dr McParland termed the 'revolutionary humaneness' of his approach to the design of penitentiaries.

His work on various public buildings made Johnston a very successful and wealthy man, but it also imposed limitations on what he could do, and this may not have sat easily with his aesthetic temperament. His concentration on institutional architecture, much of which was focused on providing basic accommodation for those on whom the sunshine of life had not been generously shed, may have depressed him. Whatever the cause, he gradually withdrew from architectural work, choosing to concentrate on other interests. He had the means to put together a very fine collection of paintings, among which were a Canaletto, a Murillo and a Rubens, and he was fascinated too by the intricacy and delicate formation of shells. His interest in bell-ringing, the peal that he rang in his garden being left to St George's, may not always, perhaps, have been appreciated locally, but his generosity in establishing and building, at his own expense, premises in Abbey Street for the Royal Hibernian Academy is testament to his devotion to and encouragement of art and culture in Dublin. The Academy, like the GPO across the street, was unfortunately destroyed in 1916. The loss of these buildings and others, like St Andrew's church in Dublin, was mirrored by the dispersal of his wonderful art collection in 1845, when it was sold at auction. It is a rather sad fate for the work of a man to whom leaving a legacy of some kind was important. Francis Johnston died in 1829 but he had largely retired from architectural work a decade before, leaving his cousin William Murray to take over his practice.

Today Johnston's plans for the GPO can be found in the Murray Collection, held in the Irish Architectural Archive. Writing to J. N. Brewer in February 1820, Johnston summarises the work he had done over his career, submitting it:

> with a due sense of the imperfections of many of my undertakings, some caused by my own inexperience and others by the whims and obstinacy of my employers, and for which I am sure you will make reasonable allowance, considering that during my life of business, the arts have advanced from a very inferior state indeed to what they now assume.[9]

The white Portland stone of the portico's Ionic columns contrasts with the darker, rougher texture of the 'mountain stone', or granite, that Johnston used for the façade. (Author's Collection)

---

9. A copy of this letter, written on 29 February 1820 from Eccles Street, was reproduced by Patrick Henchy in his article on Johnston for the *Dublin Historical Record* (1949) vol. 11, no. 1.

Few of those who walk beneath the GPO portico each day stop to admire the detailed carving on the ceiling above them, the decorated scrolls at the top of the columns and the Greek fret design, which Johnston used in several of his buildings. (Author's Collection)

Companions on Sackville Street for a century and a half, the admiral and Hibernia cast no admiring glances at each other.

It is an interesting comment that reveals not just the fundamental modesty of the man but also a canny business head, and it suggests that while he knew well how the world worked, he aspired nonetheless to something more than commerce.

The Lord Lieutenant, Lord Whitworth, laid the foundation stone of the new GPO on 12 August 1814 and £60 was spent on official entertainment for the occasion. The building, completed at a cost of £80,000, was open for business less than four years later on 6 January 1818.[10] It is by any standards a very fine Post Office and predates both Elliott and Kay's work on Edinburgh's Waterloo Place building and Sir Robert Smirke's at St Martin's le Grand in London.[11] Edinburgh's GPO was relocated in 1865, London's demolished in 1912 and, with various distinguished European postal headquarters succumbing to changed circumstances and commercial pressures over the years, Dublin's Post Office remains as one of the oldest still-functioning General Post Offices in the world.

In its general proportions and frontage, with its central portico and balustrade, there are comparisons to be made with Henry Holland's and Richard Jupp's work on the remodelled East India Company building in Leadenhall Street in London, but Johnston's final design may have been influenced more by James Gibbs' work on the hall and offices of King's College, Cambridge. Both buildings have a long three-storey façade, a central pedimented portico and a similarly distributed window and door pattern, but the Post Office's dimensions are a little smaller and the design has been simplified and made more severe by the omission of the ornamentation seen at King's. The angle of the pediment is also more acute so that it hardly rises above the roof of the building. The beauty of the whole, as John Betjeman observed in relation to Johnston's classical output, 'depends on simple vaulting and relation of window to wall space'.[12] Built of Wicklow granite, with a portico of Portland stone, the building was 223 ft long, 150 ft deep and rose 50 ft to the top of the cornice. The frontage is defined by the portico, which at 80 ft is just over a third of the total street façade, and the consequent sense of equilibrium is pleasing. The ground floor is rusticated and there are also rusticated quoins at the corners. Six Ionic columns, each 4 ft 4 inches in diameter, support the central portico, which, in what was perhaps a conscious imitation and tribute to James Gandon's work on the entrance to the House of Lords across the Liffey, spans the pavement in front of the Post Office. The original door to the public office was in

---

10. This £80,000 figure is given by Brewer and is substantially more than the £50,000 mentioned in several other contemporary accounts. Brewer, however, met Johnston when he was working on his book and acknowledged his assistance in its preface, where he thanks Francis Johnston Esq., 'the highly respected architect of the Board of Works and Civil Buildings in Ireland', who 'allowed me to encroach on much of his valuable time, and yielded me all necessary information concerning the important public structures in which he has been engaged'.

11. Smirke's Wellington Monument in the Phoenix Park dates from 1814, the same year Johnston started work on the GPO.

12. See his article on Johnston in *The Pavilion: A Contemporary Collection of British Art and Architecture*, p. 23.

This decorated cast-iron lamp base and its partner at the other end of the GPO portico are all that remain of the original railings and lamp stands that graced the GPO. Gates, which were locked at night, allowed access to the common hall entered from beneath the portico. (Author's Collection)

the central ground-floor bay under the portico and through it one entered a hall from which there were openings left and right to the offices of the General and Penny Post establishments respectively, with 'receivers', or letter boxes, for posting letters. A bay at the back of this common hall led on through to the mail-coach courtyard at the rear of the building.

Railings, set back a few feet from the façade in order to allow light into the basement rooms, ran along the front of the building, and gates, which could be locked at night, secured the area under the portico. Two fluted cast-iron lamp-stand pillars, which can still be found in front of the portico's columns, are all that remain of this ironwork today. A handsome balustrade runs above the cornice and the façade is crowned by three fine, symbolic statues, which survey the street from their commanding position above the pediment. The sculptor was John Smyth, son of Edward Smyth who carved the Custom House's famous riverine heads that once adorned our bank notes. In the centre, Hibernia stands proudly with her harp, with Fidelity, the cardinal virtue of any postal service, on her left and Mercury, the winged messenger of the gods, on her right. The current statues are copies, the originals, heavily weathered and damaged by years of city pollution, having been removed during cleaning and restoration work undertaken in 1990. Other stone carving was executed by Richard Stewart,whom Johnston would have known from their collaboration on St George's and the Chapel Royal in Dublin Castle. The entablature is highly decorated and based on an acanthus leaf pattern, a leaf that also adorns another beautiful Post Office creation – J. W. Penfold's hexagonal pillar box.

A clock was mounted in a rectangular space under the portico of the GPO, and to its left and right were others, set to give the expected times of arrival and departure of the packet ships, a useful piece of information for Dublin's citizens. The original GPO clock of 1818 or thereabouts chimed on the quarter hour and struck on the hour, using a collection of bells that weighed from 1.5 tons to 3 tons. The GPO clock gradually became part of Dublin life, its chime a reminder of a

Carved by John Smyth, the statues on the roof of the GPO embody the spirit and virtues of the Post Office. Hibernia, in the centre, represents Ireland while Fidelity, on her left with a faithful dog at her side, holds the key that symbolises trust. Hermes (Mercury in the Roman pantheon) stands on Hibernia's right, and carries the caduceus, the serpent-entwined staff that symbolises his authority as messenger of the gods.

rendezvous or a summons to get something done. Francis Johnston, himself a keen bell-ringer, may have taken a close interest in the construction and installation of the GPO bells. When in later years the six o'clock chime sounded, it signalled the shutting of the letter-box apertures at the front of the building and the imposition of a penny surcharge for anyone posting after that time. The author of one contemporary verse put it rather well:

> Many and many a time
> Have all – or at any rate most of us –
> Shuddered at hearing the chime
> Of six at the General Post Office.
> There have I frequently gone,
> But somehow I never met anyone
> Seemingly glad to put on
> A twopenny stamp for a penny one.[13]

In time the huge weight of the bells began to have an effect on the GPO's structure and they were dismantled in 1881 and erected instead in a clock tower at the university in Earlsfort Terrace. When that was taken down, the bells were separated and went to a couple of different

---

13. Hamilton, E., *Dublin Doggerels* (Smyth, Dublin, 1877), p. 5.

Addressed to Amsterdam, this 1858 letter missed the 6 p.m. closing of the GPO's letter boxes and has been specially franked to explain the reason that it was not sent with the usual evening dispatch.

churches, the large one to the church at Balla, County Mayo, and another to a church at Spiddal, in County Galway. The GPO got a new clock but one without a chime. This remained until 1915 when it was removed in the course of renovation work, and when the building was reopened after the 1916 Rising, the present blue-faced clock was installed. At a later stage the GPO had another bell connection through the Radio Éireann studios on the top floor. Archbishop McQuaid and the Post Office secretary, León Ó Broin, had been contemplating broadcasting the Angelus on the radio and during Holy Year, 1950, the bells of the Pro-Cathedral across the street were recorded. A controlling mechanism in the GPO, devised by a Post Office engineer, activated the bells, and a microphone installed in the cathedral belfry relayed the link back to the studios in the GPO, where they were broadcast daily at noon and 6 p.m. After a short time in operation, however, it was discovered that condensation in the Pro-Cathedral was causing a slight mistiming in the sounding of the bells. GPO engineering staff came up with a simple and elegant solution – the installation of a light bulb at the church, the heat of which would evaporate the condensation. From then on, every Saturday morning an electrician

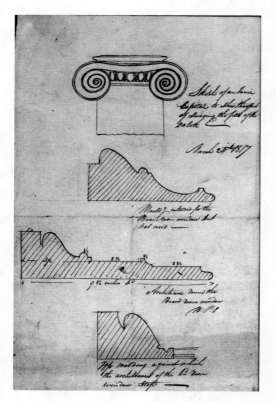

Johnston's sketches, dated 24 March 1817, which show details of his thinking for the capital of the Ionic capital and also possibilities for the window moulding of the boardroom. (Courtesy of the Irish Architectural Archive)

The kitchen was located on the Prince's Street side of the GPO. Also at basement level were the laundry, pantry and sleeping quarters for the female servants. (Courtesy of the Irish Architectural Archive)

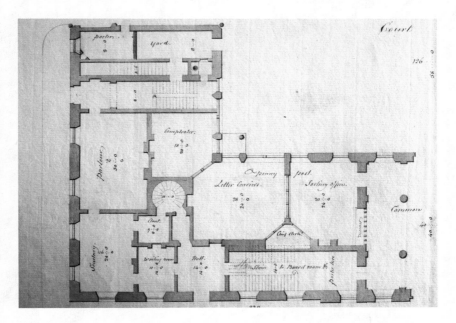

This detail of the south-east corner of the GPO shows the separate entrance to the secretary's house from Sackville Street, the hall and waiting room and spiral staircase to his private apartments. From the left of the public entrance hall under the portico, a stairway, guarded by a porter, leads up to the boardroom, and at ground level is the Penny Post Office. (Courtesy of the Irish Architectural Archive)

from the GPO would cross the road and install a new bulb to ensure the call to prayer was announced as it should be. When Radio Éireann left the GPO and went to Donnybrook, this 'live' broadcasting ended, but the building's connection with accurate time was maintained a little longer through Antoinette Rock, a former GPO telephonist, who won a competition to become the voice of Telecom Éireann's popular speaking-clock service.

This Henry Street elevation of the GPO, showing its age a little but initialled and dated November 1814 by Francis Johnston, shows the original fenestration and the gateway to the coach yard. (Courtesy of the Irish Architectural Archive)

The Henry Street elevation of November 1814 shows a three-storey over basement structure, with the ground floor of rusticated stone having an entrance archway for coaches, towards the back of the building. The windows are evenly distributed with eight on each of the upper floors and one ground-floor window replaced by the coach yard entrance. At basement level, five arched windows allow light into the kitchen and storage areas below the building. An elegant Portland stone spiral staircase culminates in an arch leading into the lobby on the second floor, a feature used by Johnston to good effect in his work elsewhere. The basement plan shows a coal vault, servants' hall, sleeping quarters for the female servants, a laundry and a room in the corner for the housekeeper. Internally the GPO was designed as a functional place of work and business and there is, in the surviving plans, very little evidence of any decorative detail. Johnston's style is severe, pared down and minimalist but there are a few touches that show he did care about ornamentation and was capable of executing ornamentation when it was called for. He has a nice drawing of one of the Ionic capitals under the portico where he notes the graceful effect of the curl on the volute. His background as the son of a builder meant that he understood the practical concerns of the men he employed. There is, for instance, a detailed instruction in the margin of the plan concerning the impost for the entrance arcade under the portico in which he notes:

> The drip not to be cut on this impost until after it is set, as the arches must set before the projection line in some places.[14]

The boardroom, located on the first floor overlooking the courtyard at the rear of the building, was furnished with two seats, one for each postmaster general, but because the secretary generally managed to run the business without the inconvenience of board meetings, there was never actually an occasion when both men were there to occupy them. Wright singled out the room as 'a very handsome apartment', and surviving architectural drawings indicate that Johnston experimented with ideas for various types of architrave mouldings here. A white marble bust of Lord Whitworth, who had laid the foundation stone, stood on the boardroom chimney piece, protected by a curtain of green silk. We know it survived until 1916 because a pencil drawing of the bust, shown resting on a fine fireplace in the secretary's office, was made just a few years before the Rising.

Brewer, looking at the finished work with the impartial eye of an outsider, gave what must have been a fair and complimentary assessment of the new Post Office. 'The building is,' he said, 'at once commodious, well arranged for the dispatch of business, and highly ornamental to the city.'[15] Johnston, a careful and thoughtful architect who, before he gave free rein to his own creative vision, did his best to understand the requirements of his clients, would have been happy with that judgement. He knew criticism too, of course. James Sadler of Moore Street, who had been engaged to install gas lighting in the GPO, was put out that he had not received full payment for his work and he wrote to the chief secretary in Dublin Castle complaining

---

14. Irish Architectural Archive (IAA) Murray Collection.

15 Brewer (1825) p. 88.

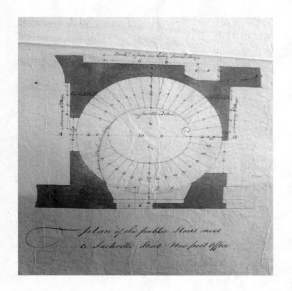
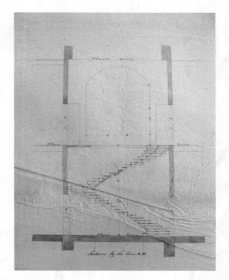

Johnston often made good use of spiral staircases. The rotunda and staircase at Townley Hall (left) is exquisite, while the use of a similar feature at the GPO must have been purely utilitarian. In a nod towards elegance, however, Johnston directed that the stone for the upper flights in the Post Office should be of Portland stone, while granite would serve for the basement. (Staircase plans: courtesy of the Irish Architectural Archive. Townley Hall: courtesy of Paddy Clarke)

of Johnston's interference in the matter. Sadler conceded that Johnston might be 'a good architect' but went on to argue that this did 'not make him competent to judge of Gas Light' and that 'the manner in which the Lamp Irons were constructed at the Post Office is a proof of how inadequate Mr Johnston is to judge of Gas Light.'[16] Perhaps, however, Johnston was a better judge than he thought, for *The Freeman's Journal* of 22 October 1880 reports on a gas leak and explosion at the GPO the previous day, when pedestrians in Sackville Street had seen 'a sudden flash of light through a window of the building, and a large bundle of papers … immediately afterwards shot violently into the street.' Fortunately no one was hurt and the workman who had been searching for the leak emerged unscathed but without his whiskers.

This sketch of the fireplace in the secretary's office was made a few years before the destruction of 1916. The bust is of Lord Whitworth, Lord Lieutenant, who laid the foundation stone of the GPO on 12 August 1814.

16 National Archives of Ireland (NAI) CSO/RP/1819/1071.

GENERAL POST OFFICE,

20th June, 1825.

WHEREAS Informations have been received on Oath, that on **TUESDAY** Morning the 14th of June Instant, whilst **FELIX MAGENNIS**, one of the Letter-Carriers of the General Post Office, was delivering his Letters on the North-Wall, he was **Violently Assaulted** by **Three Men,** at present unknown. **NOTICE IS HEREBY GIVEN,** that whoever will apprehend and **Convict,** or cause to be apprehended and **Convicted,** any of said Persons who so Assaulted the Letter-Carrier aforesaid, will be entitled to

£20 REWARD,

And if any Person whether an accomplice in said Outrage, or knowing thereof, will give such private information as may lead to the discovery of any of said Persons, such Person will not only be entitled to said Reward of £20 but the Strictest Secrecy observed, and all Expences of the Prosecution defrayed by this Office.

By Command of the Postmasters-General,

EDWARD S. LEES, Secretary.

THOM and JOHNSTON, Printers to his Majesty's Post Office.

This 1825 reward notice indicates that the job of GPO letter carrier was certainly not without its dangers.

OPPOSITE: *This attractive engraving produced by Chambers and Hallagan, stationers and printers of Abbey Street, borrows Mercury and Fidelity from the roof of the GPO to create a garlanded inscription space.*

GENERAL POST OFFICE

The Post Office, of course, has always worked closely to schedules – the arrival of mails by packet ship or coach and their efficient dispatch depended on strict adherence to accurate time-keeping – and this meant that staff had to be available for duty, sometimes at short notice. John-ston consequently designed the building to provide living accommodation for a complement of GPO staff. A House of Commons return of 1826 lists twenty-eight sorting office clerks who were provided with a 'sleeping room' in the GPO.[17] It was, however, not much more than a place to lie down. There were complaints from some of the men that their pigeonholes, 9 ft long by 6 ft wide and arranged in rows, were mere 'bird cages'. They lacked a fireplace and, in some cases, a window, and were equipped with just the barest of essentials – a water jug and a halfpenny candle.

This drawing of a possible drum cupola, inspired perhaps by the Custom House, was prepared not long after the completion of Johnston's GPO and forms part of the Murray Collection. (Courtesy of the Irish Architectural Archive)

The position was rather more comfortable for a small number of senior staff who were provided with accommodation in the GPO as part of their remuneration. Top of the list was the Post Office secretary who had been provided with a separate house for himself and his family beside the old GPO in College Green and this arrangement was continued in Sackville Street. Sir Edward Lees was very well provided for, having what was described as 'a distinct house in

---

17. House of Commons Parliamentary Papers, *Returns relating to The General Post Office, Dublin:* 6 April 1826.

the South-east wing of the building'.[18] The apartments provided for him contained space for grooms, servants and dressing rooms, and he had a kitchen, servants' hall, pantry and cellars in the basement. He and his family, eight people in total, lived above the shop in comfort and some style and had a separate front door on Sackville Street to the left of the GPO portico. A spiral staircase led from this hallway to Sir Edward's private accommodation upstairs and while no detail remains of how the architect designed the internal rooms, it is reasonable to assume that a man of Sir Edward's taste and standing insisted on a degree of decoration that would not have been found in the more functional chambers of the GPO. Henry Warren's picture of the welcome given to George IV on the occasion of the royal visit in August 1821 shows the King's carriage passing the GPO and the windows of Sir Edward's private apartments flung open to provide a wonderful vantage point as the King graciously acknowledges the cheers of his loyal Irish subjects who have been led to hope for better times under the recently crowned monarch.

Edward Baynes, who was controller of the Penny Post Office, the separate postal delivery service that operated in Dublin's city centre, was allocated four rooms in the GPO, excluding kitchen and cellarage in the basement, for himself and his family. Similar provision was made for Frederick Homan, controller of the British Mail Office, who had a large family of ten to look after, and John Burrowes, the minute clerk, was given three rooms, including a nursery, for his family. Each of these men was also given an annual allowance of coal and candles, '15 ton of coals and 18 dozen of mould candles'. These arrangements are in keeping with the responsibilities of these men, and the accommodation provided for them was an important part of their overall remuneration. What does excite some surprise is the extent of the accommodation allowed to Anne Draper, the GPO housekeeper. While the architect's 1814 basement plan shows a room for the housekeeper in the south-east corner of the GPO, not far from the sleeping accommodation allotted to the female servants, she and her family ended up with four rooms and an office on the second floor, next to the apartments of the secretary himself. Her duties comprised the domestic management of the building, but she seems to have exercised an influence and authority within the GPO that transcended the rather modest power normally associated with housekeeping responsibilities and on that subject more shall be said a little later.

To the rear of the main structure, at the back of the coach yard, was a range of single-storey ancillary buildings comprising water closets, an engine house for the fire engines, a room for the mail-coach guards, some additional office space for the secretary, Sir Edward Lees and, at the Henry Street gateway, a room that was very important for the Post Office during this period – the armoury. Attacks on the mail-coaches were frequent. Indeed one such attack was the signal for the start of the Great Rebellion of 1798, and reward notices held in An Post's archive give

---

18. *Ibid*.

clear evidence of the extent of attacks on and robberies from postal staff in the early nineteenth century. Mail-coach guards were provided with a selection of weapons – flintlock pistols, swords and generally a blunderbuss – from the GPO armoury.

Sir Edward's private coach house and stable were incorporated as part of the main building below the sleeping accommodation provided for some of the staff. This arrangement was found to be unsatisfactory, and when the postmasters general recommended the purchase of some additional property in 1822 – a piece of ground behind the GPO known as Drevar's Yard – a new and separate coach house with stable was built for him. By 1826 the main Post Office yard had been enlarged through this purchase, and more room was allowed for the dispatch of mails to the coaches. A boundary wall was also erected on the Prince's Street side of the GPO, the aim being to ensure the security of the building as much as possible and to insulate it from what was seen as 'the dangerous concerns of an extended cooperage' that adjoined the building.[19]

In designing the new GPO, Johnston had first to understand the essential working arrangements of the Post Office in Dublin: the collection, sorting and taxing of domestic and foreign mails, the role of the mail-coaches and also the newspaper business that was carried on in a private capacity by some of the GPO staff. He also had to deal with what may have been somewhat delicate personal relationships within the walls of the GPO and make practical domestic plans that accommodated the day-to-day needs of the staff and their families. Dealing with the Post Office secretary, Sir Edward Lees, on the details of the GPO plans cannot have been easy. What little is known of Johnston's personal character and temperament suggests a man rather modest and retiring in disposition, scholarly in his recreations and attached to a peaceable home life. He had no children and Cregan's portrait of Johnston and his wife in the company of his nephews is a touching one and seems to capture the soul of a sensitive, almost melancholy man. Lees, in comparison, was very much a man of the world, unquestionably polite, educated and charming but also suave, calculating and attuned to every political nuance. His portrait, in contrast, radiates confidence and a nature that seems proud, self-regarding and a touch imperious. The building, which emerged from the discussions that must have regularly taken place between these two men, in a sense reflects both personalities: while the GPO stands proudly on O'Connell Street and its massive portico dominates the surrounding streetscape, it is nonetheless reserved and correct in its regard as if Johnston's restraint has just managed to curb Sir Edward's self-importance.

---

19. *Ibid.*

Place and
Patronage

On the next morning I called on the Secretary of the Irish Post Office, and learned from him that Colonel Maberly had sent a very bad character with me ... that he was informed that I was worthless, and must in all probability be dismissed.

Anthony Trollope's first day at the GPO

Even though Ireland had lost its legislative independence by the Act of Union in 1800, the Post Office managed to maintain its independence from the rest of the United Kingdom until 1831. For nearly fifty years, in fact, the Irish Post Office managed its own affairs with only occasional reference to the authorities in London. It had its own postmaster general, two of them actually, who nominally controlled the postal business, but the day-to-day power lay in the hands of the senior official in the GPO, the Post Office secretary. Throughout this period, the position of secretary was held by just two men, Sir John Lees and later his son, Sir Edward Lees. Sir John, a Scot who had come to Ireland in the retinue of the Marquis of Townshend when he was appointed Lord Lieutenant in 1767, had served with the army and then made a successful career as an administrator on the civil side of government. He carved out for himself a niche in the Post Office and made himself indispensable there as a person whose position gave him access to information that was essential for a government that faced war

abroad and rebellion at home. By placing his relations and friends in various GPO jobs, he built up his influence and a network of contacts that served him well and, by having his son appointed to act jointly with him, ensured that the family's position would be preserved after his death. His son, Sir Edward, was also a man of enterprise, ability and a certain cunning but, unlike his father, he had not had to forge his own destiny and he perhaps lacked his father's subtle approach to strategy and awareness of the necessity for compromise.

With one brother, Thomas, installed as chief clerk and another, the Rev. Sir Harcourt, a prominent churchman and political pamphleteer who was accustomed to using the GPO and its facilities for his writing and correspondence, Sir Edward Lees and his extended family managed to retain tight control over the GPO, rewarding friends and confounding enemies, despite the efforts of postmasters general and various government commissions to introduce a system of greater transparency and accountability. The fact that Sir Edward and other Post Office staff lived in the GPO meant that business and pleasure, personal and private lives were inevitably intertwined, and little details of conduct and behaviour were scrutinised for information that might be turned to someone's advantage at some stage or other. One source in particular, a scarce pamphlet written by a savagely witty but seriously disgruntled GPO clerk, serves to illustrate Sir Edward's domain, where the influence of place, patronage and power often determined success or failure. Central to his tale is Mrs Draper, the GPO housekeeper.

Anne Draper had been appointed housekeeper in 1814 on the death of the previous incumbent, Mrs Fortescue, at a salary of £100 per annum. While her predecessor had operated with a staff of just two housemaids, Mrs Draper was provided with eight to assist her in her work, in addition to two firelighters and two lamplighters. While the building was considerably larger than the old GPO in College Green and some increase in staff must have been justified, expenditure on domestic management in the new GPO amounted, it was claimed, to more than the cost of the twenty-seven postal clerks who were obliged to stay in the GPO as part of their work. The author of this observation, it must be noted, was a clerk, Patrick O'Neill, who had fallen foul of Mrs Draper and who found, to his cost, that she had a very powerful friend in the GPO, none other than the secretary himself, Sir Edward Lees. This can only have strengthened the power already exercised by a woman who, if the following well-turned description is accurate, must have been a formidable adversary:

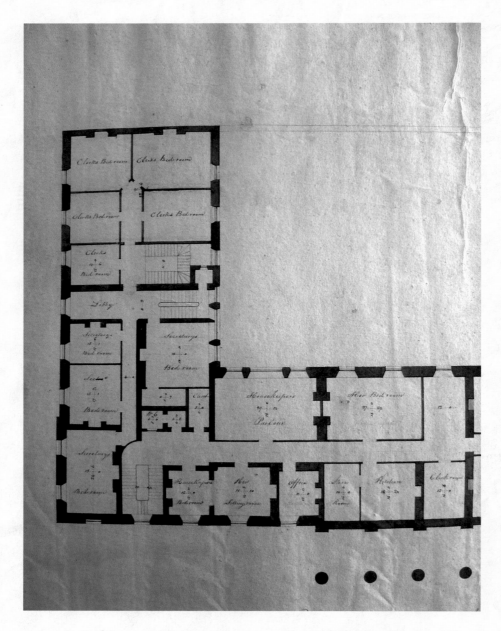

A detail of the accommodation arrangements provided for the families of the Post Office secretary and the GPO's housekeeper. (Courtesy of the Irish Architectural Archive)

OPPOSITE: *Lady Jane Lees, wife of Sir Edward.*

Mrs Draper was of a presuming and commanding disposition, and acted almost as she pleased within the walls. An Eastern Sultana could not have manifested more openly the sense of uncontroullable [*sic*] power or influence enjoyed than she displayed in it, or would have exercised it more sensibly over the whole department.[1]

The precise relationship between Mrs Draper and Sir Edward remains a matter of quiet speculation but it must have been a close one. She was 'comely as well as gay, and innocently endearing' while he was considered 'the practical *beau ideal* of fascination by that lovelier of the sexes which claims to be the judge beyond appeal of the "finished man"'.[2] Mr Draper was a good, quiet sort of man, given to oblige, and as O'Neill coyly puts it, 'exempt from the vulgar little passions of suspicion, envy and jealousy', so that he, Sir Edward and Mrs Draper 'seemed made for enjoying the society of each other'. Enjoyment of each other's company was doubtless the explanation advanced by GPO wits when they observed:

> the ingenuity of the Housekeeper in breaking a door through a middle wall, in order to facilitate the communication interiorly, between her own residence and the apartments of the Secretary, where a door had never before been thought of as requisite for the purpose of any correspondence known to the *Law-merchant*.[3]

Perhaps the fact that Stephen Draper had been employed for many years in providing ferry-boat services for the Post Office and continued to benefit from other little jobs and emoluments sent his way by his friend, Sir Edward, endowed him with the sort of equanimity that allowed him to rise above the innuendo, embarrassment and jealousy that might have afflicted lesser men. Sir Edward's wife, Jane Clarke, whom he had married in 1821, may indeed have been his second wife, for there is evidence that he had separated from a lady going under the title of Sophia, Countess Annesley, in 1811.[4]

O'Neill, finding one day some £30 worth of clothing stolen from his own very modest bedroom, complained to the secretary, outlining his view of the general domestic mismanagement in the building. His action led to 'deep-rooted resentment and hatred against me with the Supporter of the Housekeeper'. Whether his complaint on this occasion went so far as to allege that some of Mrs Draper's domestic staff were 'women of loose character, and sometimes notorious ill-fame', a circumstance which may well have led to the admission of 'equally ill-conducted followers of such persons' to the GPO, he certainly paints a picture of life

---

1. O'Neill, P. C., *A Brief Review of the Irish Post Office 1784–1831* (1831), p. 50.
2. *Ibid.*, p. 44.
3. *Ibid.*, p. 49.
4. Bayley-Butler, 'John and Edward Lees' in *The Dublin Historical Record* (1953) vol. 13, nos. 3 and 4.

at the GPO that contrasts sharply with the Victorian view of its staff as sober, pedestrian chaps for whom public service always outweighed private pleasure.

The biting satire that is to be seen in Patrick O'Neill's attack on Sir Edward's position in the GPO is very different from the formal and polite tone of the official investigations into the Irish Post Office carried out by the gentlemen who comprised the various Commissions of Enquiry appointed by the government to consider the management of various revenue-generating Irish public bodies in the opening decades of the nineteenth century. However, the government report makes no attempt to hide the bewildered surprise of the various commissioners and British Post Office officials appointed to carry out the enquiry. That their criticisms so often seemed to have been anticipated and shared by Sir Edward Lees, the very man whom they might reasonably have expected to instigate necessary improvements, must have baffled if not vexed them. His unfailing courtesy, willingness to assist them in their work and apparent readiness to accept recommendations for improvement to his department, however, ensured that enquiries into the Irish way of doing things in the GPO extended over two decades and generated hundreds of pages of evidence. What emerges is the picture of an institution that, to cast it in modern terms, lacks a robust system of corporate governance. The patient examination of various senior GPO officials on matters of auditing and general financial procedure elicits answers that bring to mind the exchanges at more recent public tribunals and enquiries in Ireland. Here, for example, is John Burrowes of the Secretary's Office being questioned on how a particular GPO fund is managed:

The stern sobriety of the GPO's façade preserves an honourable silence on the domestic dramas and romantic assignations it has witnessed over the years.

Question: You neither directly nor indirectly know any thing of the mode in which the proceeds of this fund are appropriated, independent of the payment to the clerks who do the duty?

Answer: No; I might accidentally hear of this or the other sum being paid, but I have no possible means of ascertaining it accurately; there might be various payments made out of that fund, of which I know nothing.[5]

Burrowes, however, is straightforward and helpful in his answers compared with his boss, Sir Edward Lees, who was examined about other accounts that were 'so involved and confused that it is impossible to explain them without further information'. This the commissioners duly

124.	First Junior Sorter	Edward Darley -	- - d° - in 1805 -
125.	Second Junior Sorter	Alexander Mitchell -	- - d° - in 1816 -
	MAIL COACH OFFICE:		
126.	Surveyor and Superintendent.	Joseph Ferguson -	- by postmasters general in 1808.
127.	Assistant ditto - -	Patrick Urquhart -	- - d° - in 1812 -
128.	Clerk - - - -	Thomas Usher -	- - d° - in 1814 -
	SHIP LETTER OFFICE:		
129.	Collector and First Clerk.	John L. Draper -	- by postmasters general in 1819.
130.	Second Clerk - -	James Clarke -	- - d° - in 1821 -
	BYE and DEAD LETTER OFFICE:		
131.	Superintendent and Clerk of the Ulster Road.	William Johnson -	- by postmasters general in 1777.
132.	First Clerk - -	John Hebden -	- - d° - in 1804 -

This excerpt from the 1829 House of Commons enquiry is indicative of the thorough investigation made into the operations of the Irish Post Office in the early nineteenth century.

5. *Commissioners of Inquiry into Collection and Management of Revenue in Ireland and Great Britain: nineteenth report* (Post Office Revenue – Ireland) with appendix p. 599: Examination of Mr John Burrowes, 20 October 1823.

sought from him, but his replies, which seemed to blend disarming honesty with a sweeping superciliousness, must have left his interrogators quite perplexed:

Question: Do you periodically audit that account?

Answer: Never, I never look at it.

Question: Have you ever looked at the account?

Answer: I never have in my life.

Question: Does it appear to you that that is the way to conduct a public account?

Answer: I do not regard that as a public account by any means.

Question: What account do you call it?

Answer: It always went by the name of the Suspension Fund.

Question: Is it not an account relating to individuals employed by the public?

Answer: So far it is, but I do not call it a public account, for I do not consider the money as public money.[6]

Questioning continues in this vein, with Sir Edward telling the commissioners that it is his brother Thomas who acts as chief clerk and who would, he is sure, be 'much obliged to you for recommending its abolition' as it is such a nuisance to look after. All sums, of course, are properly vouched for, maintains the secretary, which prompts a dry remark from the commissioners as to the number of vouchers being 'probably very extensive'. Undaunted, Sir Edward coolly replies, 'Yes; I dare say there is a press full of them' and says he 'would not take the charge of that book for the value of it; it is an invidious sort of account to have the management of'.[7] For Sir Edward it was, in truth, a wonderful account and, with his brother technically in charge of it, he was able to use it as he wished and at the same time distance himself from its management.

There certainly were vouchers and receipts, of course, many approved by one or other of the postmasters general and there was undoubtedly disbursement for legitimate Post Office business, whether it was compensation for items lost, pensions in hardship cases or entertainment on special occasions. There was, however, no proper bookkeeping system and this allowed money to be diverted to private expenditure for the benefit of the secretary, his family and friends. What had begun, many years earlier, as a small emergency fund for petty incidents had grown into a substantial account that imposed hefty fines on staff and mail-coach contractors whose performance was judged unsatisfactory. Its continuation served not only the Lees family but other senior GPO officials who received a percentage of the fines imposed. It was in no way a secret system, for the postmasters general knew of it and often sanctioned payments, but they

---

6. *Ibid.*, p. 528: Examination of Sir Edward Lees, 17 October 1823.

7. *Ibid.*, p. 529.

did not exercise day-to-day control over the account, and the lack of any regular audit meant it could be used for everything from secret service payments to a new pianoforte for Sir Edward's apartments or hiring a military band to entertain the Grand Duke Michael of Russia when he visited Dublin.

The fact that Sir Edward Lees and some of his officials underwent what was a testing investigation by the Commissioners of Enquiry and emerged largely unruffled may well be attributed to the fact that he had gone through all this before, some years earlier. The very same financial and administrative weaknesses that were highlighted in 1823 had been the subject of negative comment back in 1809. Various accounting deficiencies in the Treasurer's Office and the Accountant General's Office had been identified, with the same person conducting the business in both offices:

> the principal in neither doing any duty, and consequently the benefit that might be derived from the check the former was intended to maintain upon the latter was entirely lost.[8]

The enquiry went on to consider the position of those at the very top of the Post Office, the Irish postmasters general, and to impress upon them the need for greater attention to daily business. It was a peculiarity of the Irish Post Office that the role of postmaster general was shared between two people, noblemen whose interests, both personal and political, meant that they were generally not in Dublin and often out of the country altogether. During their absence from Dublin, it is not surprising that the business of the Post Office should have come to be controlled by the secretary, whose orders soon came to be 'acted upon and held as valid as those of the Postmaster General'.[9] In these circumstances, the need for the Office of Postmaster General itself was questioned, but the report conceded that good management required 'the existence of a paramount superintending authority' to the lack of which it attributed:

> the accumulation of errors in the Accounts, the frequent embezzlement of private property, and the delay and irregularity in the conveyance and delivery of the Mails ... so long and so loudly complained of by the Public.[10]

This is strong criticism of GPO management – criticism which, it must in fairness be said, was also being levelled at the postal authorities in London at this time. It is true that some

---

8. *The Ninth Report of the Commissioners Appointed to Enquire into the Fees, Gratuities, Perquisites, and emoluments, which are or have been lately received in certain Public Offices in Ireland – General Post-Office*, p. 11.

9. *Ibid.*, p. 25.

10. *Ibid.*, p. 26.

Laurence Parsons, 2nd Earl of Rosse, was appointed Irish postmaster general in 1809, acting jointly with Charles O'Neill, 1st Earl O'Neill. His efforts to implement a greater degree of executive control over Post Office operations were hampered by the nature of his joint appointment. (Courtesy of the Earl and Countess of Rosse)

improvements were made. Lord Clermont, one of the postmasters general in 1809, took the commission's recommendations to heart and did try to implement changes. Lord Rosse was also active and endeavoured to check the extent of the secretary's *de facto* power, but overall it is clear that tradition, vested interests and lethargy prevailed to such an extent that the same drama, with the same leading actors and some new faces among the supporting cast, was replayed on a number of occasions over the next twenty years or so. In the end, however, even Sir Edward's winning combination of charm, connections and cunning had to succumb to pressure for reform within Dublin's GPO and, faced with possible dismissal, he opted in 1831 to swop positions with his opposite number in Edinburgh, Augustus Godby. His departure from the GPO removed a colourful character from the Dublin scene and, while he had a rather flexible interpretation of the distinction between his private affairs and his public employment, his role in extending the post office network, in defending the particular interest of the Irish Post Office when it did not coincide with that of Britain and in the construction of the GPO, deserves recognition.

The continuing independence of the Irish Post Office for many years after the Act of Union owes much to the canny shrewdness of the Lees family and their friends in the GPO. Desire to keep their hands close to a steady income stream and to maintain their status and influence were motivating factors in what they did, but Sir John Lees, who had built his family's position on the GPO, had been an able administrator who had cultivated political contacts and made himself a useful agent of government in Ireland. Before the adoption of major postal reforms in the early Victorian era, employment in the GPO offered opportunities for legitimate private gain in a way that would not be countenanced a few years later. The Lees administration certainly stretched what was an already generous understanding of public service at the time, but business that today would be seen as unquestionably private and at odds with public sector employment was not merely tolerated but encouraged. Nowhere can this be more clearly seen than in the newspaper-distribution business that, with government sanction, was dominated by senior GPO officials not only in Dublin but also in London. In order to appreciate just how this curious mixture of public and private enterprise flourished within Dublin's GPO, it is helpful to have some understanding of the infrastructure of the Irish postal system at the time.

The routing or circulation of mail in Ireland has always been broadly based on two principal factors: the road network and the post town. From its earliest days the Post Office recognised three 'great roads' in the sense of primary postal divisions – south to Cork, west to Galway and north to Belfast and Derry. These roads were overseen by four Post Office employees – an additional Leinster road, overseen by the Post Office secretary himself, was subsequently created – who were designated clerks of the roads. Originally, these clerks had been responsible for the sorting and dispatch of the mail into their respective roads but by the later eighteenth century this work was done by other staff, the titles and benefits being attached instead to senior officials in the GPO. In the early nineteenth century the number of primary postal divisions was increased but this had no effect on the clerks of the roads, whose positions were by then firmly bound to the exercise of a particular benefit – the right to circulate, free of postage charges, Irish newspapers throughout the land. This valuable benefit had its origins in the seventeenth century and had grown steadily more lucrative with the growth in the number of newspaper titles. There was substantial extra money to be made from this business, and the positions, which were awarded on the basis of seniority, were eagerly anticipated by men who put up with long years of service on modest salaries in the hope of eventually gaining one of the plum jobs.

While the GPO's clerks of the roads controlled the distribution of Irish newspapers, their enterprise did not extend to British papers. This was the preserve of the express clerks, the two most senior clerks in the Inland Office, the senior of whom was Ambrose Leet. He managed the business in conjunction with his junior colleague, Stephen De Joncourt, a member of a Dundalk Huguenot family, which had supplied a number of employees to the Post Office. These men, with due official sanction, were permitted to manage for their own profit the circulation of British periodicals and lottery lists in Ireland. The newspapers, specially marked and bundled by Post Office clerks in London, would be brought across the Irish Sea on the mail boats and conveyed with all speed to the GPO in Dublin. The Dublin express clerks would then check the stock and send off the papers to their Irish subscribers by the next post.

Distribution was by the mail-coaches, which had been introduced to Ireland in 1789, some five years after they had been pioneered in England on the Bristol to London road. Because the coaches left from the GPO, the clerks running the newspaper-distribution business had a definite advantage over the newspaper proprietors in that they could insert their papers up to the very last moment, long after posting facilities had been closed to the public. There were even suspicions that Post Office staff sometimes deliberately delayed papers being dispatched by those outside their own circle through a practice called 'fishing', whereby they checked to see if any unpaid correspondence had been hidden within the folds of the newspapers. In the course of one parliamentary enquiry into the matter, one newspaper man, Alexander Johnston, whose family firm would eventually supplant the express clerks, had this to say on the subject:

> *Question:* Do you find your business as a newspaper vender much interfered with by the privileges of the express clerks?
>
> *Answer:* Very much; they were in direct hostility to us when we commenced, Mr Leet particularly.
>
> *Question:* In what way was that shown?
>
> *Answer:* Papers that came to us, that did not come through them, they used to open, consequently they were retarded in their delivery; they used to retard the delivery of them, pretending they had a right to open them to see whether there were any letters.[11]

On another occasion, allegations were made that Leet, tacitly supported by Sir Edward Lees, had one night refused sorting assistance to a colleague in another section of the GPO to ensure that priority delivery would be afforded to correspondence within the Leet & De Joncourt business. That matter led to the suspension of one senior official. The subsequent investigation, in the

---

11. *Commissioners of Inquiry, Nineteenth Report*, p. 737.

course of which management of the Post Office came under embarrassingly close scrutiny, involved the postmasters general and the Chief Secretary's Office. It brought to the surface the inevitable conflicts that arose when public and private interests contended for the loyalty of certain Post Office staff. It is possible to gain an insight into how this rather remarkable private business flourished within the walls of what was, after all, a public institution through correspondence addressed to Christopher Dillon Bellew of Bellewstown, Castleblakeney, County Galway.

A receipt issued to Christopher Dillon Bellew from the private newspaper- and book-distribution business run in the GPO and managed by two senior clerks, Ambrose Leet and Stephen De Joncourt. (Courtesy of the National Library of Ireland)

The Dillon Bellews, a Roman Catholic landlord family, were unusual in that during a time of anti-Catholic legislation they had managed to preserve and develop their estate over the eighteenth century. Christopher Dillon Bellew was not only an improving landlord and keen bibliophile, but also a member of Wolfe Tone's Catholic Committee who had put the case for Catholic emancipation to the King himself. His interest in politics, literature and current affairs made him just the sort of person with whom Leet & De Joncourt would have been happy to do business. Replying to his initial enquiry about their business, they wrote to him on Christmas Eve 1822:

We are favoured with your letter of 23rd inst and in reply beg to say that any order you favour us with shall be most punctually attend(*ed*) to for any period required. Periodical works ordered thro' us are forwarded to our correspondents by the first mail after publication, that is books published in London on the 1st of the month would be received by a correspondent in your part of the country on the 4th. Our newspapers have many advantages over those received thro' any other channel which you will perceive by perusing our list.[12]

The newspapers and periodicals supplied by Leet reflect the interests of a country gentleman of a serious and intellectual disposition – the *Classical Journal*, the *Statesman*, the *Catholic Miscellany*, *Intellectual Repository* and *Farmer's Journal*. One book, *Martyrs de la Foi*, was not to be had in London, but Leet & De Joncourt undertook to apply for it through one of their French bookseller contacts. Their normal terms for London periodicals were stated to be 6½d. per number above the price the paper was sold for in London shops. Taking into account free postage within Ireland and whatever discounted terms they were able to negotiate with the London newspapers, the business was clearly a lucrative one. Their subscriber in County Galway, however, kept a close eye on their account and seems to have done his best to have a set of books delivered to him for the price of a single volume. This elicited a polite but firm response from Messrs Leet & De Joncourt:

In our letter to you on the subject of charges we stated that 6½d per book above the London shop price was our usual terms. By book we could not mean other than volume, as it could not be supposed if a work contained eight or more volumes that it would be forwarded from London to Castleblakeney for 6½d or on the same terms that we could send one volume.[13]

While the argument may have shifted to e-mail and Amazon, the discussion may strike a familiar chord with the book collectors and dealers of our own time!

By early 1824 Ambrose Leet's name had disappeared from the crescent-shaped Leet & De Joncourt frank that marked their business correspondence. He had been promoted to become one of the clerks of the roads, although by this stage the distinction between those positions and the express clerks had become blurred. The profits of the amalgamated Irish and British newspaper circulation business were disbursed among these six senior men. Stephen De Joncourt took over from Leet and brought in Francis Harvey, the clerk next in line, to continue this unique and fascinating little business.

Within the next few years, however, there would be changes in the GPO in Dublin. The special privileges of the Post Office clerks would be abolished under the lord-lieutenancy of the

---

12. NLI, Bellew of Mount Bellew Papers, Ms. 27,315 (1).

13. *Ibid.*, Ms. 27,315 (2).

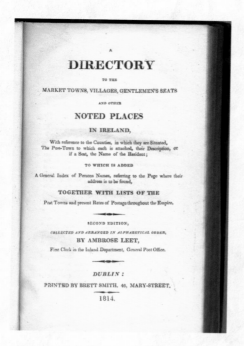

A
DIRECTORY
TO THE

MARKET TOWNS, VILLAGES, GENTLEMEN'S SEATS

AND OTHER

NOTED PLACES

IN IRELAND,

With reference to the Counties, in which they are Situated,
The Post-Town to which each is attached, their Description, or
if a Seat, the Name of the Resident;

TO WHICH IS ADDED

A General Index of Persons Names, referring to the Page where their
address is to be found,

TOGETHER WITH LISTS OF THE

Post Towns and present Rates of Postage throughout the Empire.

SECOND EDITION,

COLLECTED AND ARRANGED IN ALPHABETICAL ORDER,
BY AMBROSE LEET,
First Clerk in the Inland Department, General Post Office.

DUBLIN:
PRINTED BY BRETT SMITH, 46, MARY-STREET,
1814.

The title page of Ambrose Leet's 1814 edition of A Directory to the Market Towns, Villages, Gentlemen's Seats and Other Noted Places in Ireland.

Duke of Richmond in favour of private newspaper and courier interests. The Irish Post Office, which, despite the Act of Union, had continued to function independently of London, would be brought back under English control, and an eighteenth-century management system, based on patronage and a flexible view of the distinction between private and public money, would be gradually brought to an end.

It is tempting to judge some of these GPO staff by the clear-cut rules regarding conflicts of interest imposed on twenty-first-century employees and to forget that the entrepreneurial spirit must accommodate itself to the standards of the age in which it finds itself. In applying just such an enterprising spirit, Ambrose Leet used his position in the GPO to secure for himself a minor but enduring reputation as the author of *A Directory to the Market Towns, Villages, Gentlemen's Seats and other Noted Places in Ireland*. Published by Brett Smith of Mary Street in 1814, it is a pioneering work that drew on the eighteenth-century precedents of Thomas Stewart and William Wilson and foreshadowed the more extensive listings that would make up the street directories of men like Pigot, Pettigrew and, of course, Thom. In compiling such a work, Leet created not only a useful marketing tool for his own newspaper business but also an invaluable database of addresses for the GPO. His project had the backing of the postmasters general themselves, who in the interests of greater knowledge and accuracy in mail delivery had graciously permitted him to receive information on omissions and corrections free of postage, the letters to be addressed to The First Clerk, Inland Department, General Post Office, Dublin, and endorsed 'Information of Noted Place'.

Ambrose Leet, who had entered the GPO in 1785, was still on its books in 1829, when he is recorded as vice-president of the Inland Office and clerk of the Connaught Road, but he must have retired soon after that date. His long and successful Post Office career, with its unique blend of public service and private enterprise, reflected the place and patronage system of the age in which he lived. It was a system that, though coming to the end of its time, had a few years left to run and would benefit one of the great literary figures of the nineteenth century, Anthony Trollope.

Trollope is well known as a novelist and as creator of several memorable characters in his Barsetshire and Palliser books, but few are aware that he was also a major figure in the Post Office, responsible for the introduction of the pillar box and for the extension of postal services to rural districts. He spent many years in Ireland and it was his move there in 1841 that saved him from likely dismissal in London. He had joined the Post Office as a clerk in 1834, through a family contact, Sir Francis Freeling, the British Post Office secretary. His sister later married a fellow clerk, John Tilley, who would also rise to the top of the Post Office establishment. Trollope, however, found the daily work of copying letters and minutes very dreary and failed to apply himself to it. He was lonely in London and when a vacancy for a surveyor's clerk arose in Ireland, he saw a chance to make a fresh start. Duly appointed by his superiors, who were glad enough to be rid of him, he sailed for Dublin on his way to take up his job in Banagher, County Offaly. His autobiography, first published in 1883, is an entertaining account of his life and work and he confesses that his understanding of what he was to do in Ireland, and of the country itself, was very vague.

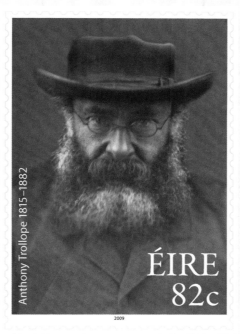

Anthony Trollope 1815–1882

ÉIRE
82c

2009

ABOVE: *Julia Margaret Cameron's 1864 albumen print, on which the stamp is based, captures the stern intensity which allowed Trollope to be both an efficient postal official and prolific novelist.*

OVERLEAF: *Drumsna, County Leitrim, on the banks of the Shannon was Anthony Trollope's base as a surveyor's clerk in 1843 and the place where he found the inspiration for his first novel,* The MacDermots of Ballycloran. *(Author's Collection)*

On 15 September 1841 Trollope arrived in Dublin:

> without an acquaintance in the country, and with only two or three letters of introduction from a brother clerk in the Post Office. I had learned to think that Ireland was a land flowing with fun and whisky, in which irregularity was the rule of life, and where broken heads were looked upon as honourable badges.

This happy vision was tempered a little when he duly reported to the GPO the following day and met Augustus Godby, the secretary, who told him he had heard a poor report of him and that 'he had been informed that I was worthless, and must in all probability be dismissed'. To his credit, however, Godby said he would judge him on his own merits and 'From that time to the day on which I left the service, I never heard a word of censure, nor had many months passed

A remarkable sense of stillness pervades this 1865 photograph by F. H. Mares, one of the earliest known shots of the GPO. (Courtesy of Davison & Associates)

Shaving, Singeing, Shampooing, and strict Cleanliness; speciality, artistic beard trimming; Gentlemen's hair cut, 3d. 2 Temple lane, Dame street.
p7873cl

FIRE! Fire!! Fire!!! James H Webb and Co, Limited, beg to apologise to the numerous customers of their Branch Establishment at 23 South George's street, for the unavoidable delay in the execution and delivery of their orders occasioned by the disastrous fire in the market buildings.

FEMALE Telegraph Learners (London); at examination held June last Miss Alice Gordon was successful direct from Skerry's Academy, Dublin; seven successes last Dublin examination.
p7799xIe

GENTLEMEN'S own materials made up; Tweed Suits made and trimmed, One Guinea; six yards of tweed sufficient. At M'Cudden's, 18 Fownes street.
p7901eg

GPO; J Cathcart and Co, Basketmakers to General Post Office, all kinds of Wicker Work made to order. Manufactury, 4 Lower Exchange street, Dublin.
p7865ck

HAND-Made Wheels of Irish Oak and Ash thoroughly seasoned in our own stores wheels repaired without delay; shoeing, Tuesdays and Fridays; good workmanship at moderate charges. Briscoe's Carriage, Van, and Wheel Works Summerhill.
p7808zIa

INN'S quay Ward Branch Irish National League Weekly Meeting will be held on Thursday, 8th inst, at 8 o'clock, in Labourers' Hall (late Foresters' Hall), 55 Bolton street.
p7898eg

INCHICORE; Cottages to Let, Park street, two-roomed, enclosed yard, at 2s and 2s 6d; Phœnix street, three-roomed, enclosed yard, 3s 6d; splendid situation. Apply Agent, 3 First avenue, Inchicore.
p7869c

Doing business with the GPO was regarded for many years as a sign of respectability, and Mr Cathcart, basketmaker, is glad to advertise the fact in this 1892 Evening Herald *advertisement.*

before I found that my services were valued' and 'I had acquired the character of a thoroughly good public servant'.[14]

While he paid regular visits to the GPO, Anthony Trollope's responsibilities in the surveying department of the Post Office meant that he spent most of his time based elsewhere in Ireland. Indeed, he travelled frequently and was assigned to different parts of Ireland and England during

---

14 Trollope, A., *An Autobiography* (Oxford University Press, Oxford, 1923), pp. 56–7.

his career. He met his wife in Dun Laoghaire, or Kingstown as it was then, and his sons, Henry Merivale and Fredric James Anthony, were born in Clonmel. From Cork to Belfast, Trollope built up a detailed knowledge of the country and came to appreciate it greatly. Some of his novels are set in Ireland and he also contributed a series of letters to a London paper, the Liberal weekly *Examiner*, on the effect of the famine in Ireland and the government's response to the disaster. Within the Post Office, respect for his expert knowledge of the Irish postal system led to his attendance as a witness in 1855 before a House of Commons select committee established to review postal arrangements in the south of Ireland. His intimate knowledge of the times and arrangements for collection and dispatch between Limerick, Cork and Waterford is impressive and was noted by his superiors, who went on to use him for special negotiations with foreign postal administrations. Despite his increasing fame in the literary world, he did not leave the Post Office to devote himself full-time to writing until 1867. His time in Ireland is fittingly remembered in the GPO Museum, where his portrait appears beside a unique pillar box, one of the first to be erected in Ireland during his time as Post Office surveyor.

It was during Trollope's time that the Post Office was transformed from a small and rather cosy department, run to a great extent on the basis of friends and influence, to an institution of national importance organised on adherence to systematic procedures and detailed rules. Yet there remained, even in later years, a special prestige in being associated with the GPO. Members of staff would sometimes add to their home addresses in street directories the words 'and GPO' as if association with that building and its work conferred an aura of superior status unavailable to ordinary mortals. Various city and national contractors would often insert their connection with the Post Office as a similar badge of distinction in their newspaper advertisements. The *Evening Herald* of 7 September 1892, for instance, carries an advertisement for J. Cathcart & Co. of 4 Lower Exchange Street, Dublin, which extols their virtues as makers of all kinds of wicker work and 'basketmakers to the GPO'. It wasn't on the same level as a royal patent, but for many ordinary businesses, their connection with the GPO was a practical sign that their workmanship and products had passed the rigorous quality tests imposed by its officials.

Creating an *Institution*

꜁ ꜀

What a wonderful man is the postman
As he hurries from door to door
What a myriad of news he holds in his hand
For high, low, rich and poor.

Popular song by L. M. Thornton, *c.* 1860

꜁ ꜀

The provision of a national postal service required a high degree of administrative efficiency and a clear organisational structure. The GPO was at the centre of this structure and, since the formation of a separate Irish Post Office in 1784, had been divided into a number of administrative and accounting departments, each with its own responsibilities. At the very top were two postmasters general, noblemen who held their appointments under letters patent and who jointly shouldered the responsibility for the Post Office. This rather odd arrangement was, not surprisingly, unwieldy and inconvenient and meant that the day-to-day management of the business lay with the Post Office secretary, whose office was consequently the real seat of power within the organisation. The manner in which that power was used gave rise, from time to time, to tension and complaint both locally and further afield. The continued existence of an Irish Post Office, independent of London's authority, for many years after the legislative

THE POSTMAN'S KNOCK QUADRILLE

Introducing the Melody of the new and favorite

Song

THE POSTMAN'S KNOCK

SONG.

London

ROBERT COCKS & Cᵒ PUBLISHERS TO HER MAJESTY QUEEN VICTORIA & THE EMPEROR NAPOLEON III.

ENT. STA. HALL

PRICE 2/6

S. ROSENTHAL LITH.

2 RED LION SQUAR HOLBORN.

Composed

for the Pianoforte

BY

STEPHEN CLOVER

(Copyright)

union of Ireland with Britain was often a cause of annoyance to senior postal officials in London, and ensured that parliamentary enquiries into the Irish Post Office were closely scrutinised by men like Sir Francis Freeling, who exercised over the British Post Office a dominion not dissimilar to that of Sir Edward Lees in Dublin. The organisational structure of the GPO in Dublin essentially mirrored the system operated in London, and the day-to-day running of the postal business would have been very familiar to any visiting London official. Closer inspection of the Dublin operation would, however, have revealed differences in responsibilities, in pay and in administrative procedures, and it was these that tended, in the early decades of the nineteenth century, to draw negative comment. The existence of the Irish Post Office as a separate entity, its smaller scale and its more intimate relationship with government officials in Dublin, meant that the increasingly vocal demands for reform within the Post Office in Britain, in terms of efficiency and rates, carried less weight in Ireland and allowed the traditional patronage system to remain in place much longer there. The political circumstances of the country, manifested in campaigns like Daniel O'Connell's drive for Catholic emancipation, the Tithe War and repeal of the Union itself, ensured that scruples over financial management, for example, would be set aside in favour of the political loyalty of public officials.

Within his office, the secretary had a small staff to assist him, the senior person being his own brother, T. O. Lees, who acted as assistant secretary and deputy in his absence. The clerks in this office dealt with daily correspondence, initiating enquiries when necessary and drafting replies for the secretary's signature. A letter from the Waterford Chamber of Commerce in 1824, for instance, sought improvements in the arrangements for transferring British mails from Dunmore, where it was landed, to Waterford. The reply was carefully drafted by a clerk in the Secretary's Office in good civil-service form and placed before Sir Edward, who added his signature. The style and language of such letters would grow less grandiloquent over the years but there is really very little to choose between Sir Edward's 'I am commanded by My Lords the Post Masters general to apprize you for the information of …' and An Rúnaí's 'I am directed by the Minister to inform you …' a century and a half later.

The tendency of a large bureaucracy like the Post Office to preserve, largely unaltered, the language, forms and structures of the past is one of its more remarkable features. Its capacity to mould and embalm those who spend their working lives in its service is amusingly captured in the title of one nineteenth-century postal autobiography, *Half-a-Century in the Dead Letter*

Office. Its author, G. R. Smith, was an Englishman who retired in 1891 at the age of seventy-three, though he 'did not feel a bit old or incapable' and who recalled a visit of inspection to the GPO's Dead Letter Office in 1859.[1] He was given a hearty welcome there and in the evening entertained at 'a refined dinner' to which the secretary, Gustavus Cornwall, had invited all the senior staff. Smith, who was an amateur photographer and had a good eye for what he thought striking or unusual, travelled in the course of his business to other places in Ireland, but it was while he was staying in a hotel close to the GPO in Sackville Street that he recorded his view of a Dublin funeral as it made its way down the street. It was a Sunday morning and he and his colleagues noticed a procession passing by.

> At the head of this line were about a dozen men wearing peaked-tail coats of green colour, brown knickers, grey stockings, and greenish hats, and some were smoking short pipes. These were followed at a little distance by two men holding, one at each end, a pole of about seventeen feet long. To this pole was slung, by two large red cotton handkerchiefs, a heavy box; just behind the hinder man came a donkey cart, in which sat three women with large coloured shawls on their heads, and then came a motley line of men, women and children, on foot, some forty or fifty of them. On close examination, and enquiry, we found the box slung to the pole was a coffin containing the body of a child.

For those in the GPO it must have been a sad but commonplace occurrence. To the eyes of their English colleagues, however, not accustomed perhaps to the display of all aspects of life and death on the principal thoroughfare of a nation's capital, 'it appeared grotesque and out of the fitness of things'.[2]

A few of the GPO men who met Smith at the dinner organised in his honour might have recalled a similar occasion many years before when a previous GPO secretary had invited a German prince, Hermann von Pückler-Muskau, to breakfast in the GPO and given him a tour of the Dead Letter Office as an appetiser. The prince's account of the tour survives in a series of letters he wrote home to his wife. It provides an interesting vignette of the workings of a pleasantly relaxed GPO in 1828.

> The Director, Sir Edward Lees, a very agreeable and accomplished man, who gave the entertainment, first conducted us, in company with a number of elegant ladies, through the various offices *'pour nous faire gagner de l'appetit'*. In one of these, called the 'Dead Letter Office', a very strange incident occurred in our presence. All letters, the address of which is unintelligible, or

---

1. Smith, G. R., *Half-a-Century in the Dead Letter Office* (W. C. Hemmons, Bristol, 1908), p. 141.
2. *Ibid*, pp. 83–4.

which are addressed to persons who cannot be discovered, are taken into this office, where they are opened at the end of a fortnight, and, if they contain nothing important, burnt. This seems to me rather a barbarous custom, since many a heart might be broken from the loss of what a Post-office clerk might think 'of no importance'. So it is however, and we found three men busied in the operation. Several of us seized these doomed epistles, and turned them over with great curiosity, when the clerk who stood nearest to me took up rather a large packet on which there was no address whatever, only the post-mark of an Irish country town. How great was his surprise and that of all of us, when on opening it we saw not a single line of writing, but £2700 in bank-notes! This at least appeared 'of importance' to all, and an order was immediately given to write to the town in question to make inquiry about it.[3]

One would be forgiven for thinking that the prince, who had only been in the country a few weeks, had already learned the Irish art of telling a good story: £2,700 does seem an extraordinary amount to have sent through the post. However, GPO archives contain a reward poster from this time seeking information in the case of a missing letter that contained £1,500 in Bank of England

GENERAL POST OFFICE,
SACKVILLE-STREET.

1844.

Post-Master-General,
RIGHT HON. VISCOUNT LOWTHER.

SECRETARY'S OFFICE.	MONEY ORDER OFFICE.
Secretary, Augustus Godby, esq.	*Chief Clerk,* Stephen W. Creaghe, esq.
Chief Clerk, Thomas Orde Lees, esq.	
Clerks, Charles Bond, John Mockler, Arthur Green, Urquhart Thompson, Henry James, and John Owen, esqrs	INLAND OFFICE.
	Superintending President.
Surveyors, Patrick Urquhart, James Kendrick and Jas. Drought, esqrs.	J. Burrowes, esq.
Surveyors' Clerks, Stephen Maberly, J. R. Vaughton, and Anthony Trollope, esqrs.	*Vice-Presidents,* J. W. Gladstone, H. Clare, and E. Darley, esqrs.

GPO departmental list of 1844. While Sir Edward Lees was replaced by Augustus Godby, his brother T. O. Lees survived as second in command at the GPO. Also listed is the novelist, Anthony Trollope. (Author's Collection)

---

3. Pückler-Muskau, H., *Tour in England, Ireland, and France in the years 1828 and 1829, Vol. II* (Effingham Wilson, London, 1832), pp. 140–1.

post bills, so it would be unjust, after all, to accuse the prince of exaggeration and the work of the Dead Letter Office, in the guise of An Post's returned letter branch, continues to this day.

Accounting and financial business was the preserve of the Treasurer's Office, which lodged remittances with the Bank of Ireland, and the Accountant General's Office, which looked after the accounts of the various postmasters throughout the country. The senior financial men at this time were gentlemen, who had other business interests besides their positions in the GPO. Robert Shaw of Terenure House, on a salary of £500, was accountant general and had prospered in business as a flour merchant, while Graves Chamney Swan, who received emoluments of £750, was partner in a legal firm. His name appears on the harbour memorial at Dun Laoghaire, where he is among those thanked for their efforts in having the new harbour built. From the obelisk on his land at Newtown Park, he might have been able to keep track of progress. Day-to-day accounting in the GPO was in the hands of clerks who, like most of the staff there, were appointed by the postmasters general on more modest salaries. Samuel Ferguson, to pick a name at random, was junior window man in the Penny Post Office on a salary of £70, while Martin Keogh and Joshua Fox, both GPO letter carriers, were on just £36 8s. each. Sir Edward Lees' total emoluments in 1822 amounted to £1,415 6s. 4d., just short of the £1,500 received by each of the postmasters general.[4]

Surveyors and their clerks were the staff who inspected post offices and implemented improvements in mails operations. In 1844 the novelist Anthony Trollope Esq. is listed as a surveyor's clerk attached to the Secretary's Office. The introduction of an official money order system in 1838 provided a cheap and much safer way of sending money through the postal system and the oversight of this business required the creation of a new Money Order Office in the GPO.[5] While the Post Office advocated the use of money orders as a low-cost, secure and convenient method of remitting money, it recognised that people do not always adopt new schemes easily, and in a notice to the public it continued to recommend that bank notes and cheques 'should be cut in halves, and the second halves should not be despatched until after the receipt for the first has been acknowledged'. A Mail-coach Office also remained, until the move to railways, an important part of the GPO's administrative structure, of course. The coaches would enter the GPO yard by the south entrance gate and, having delivered or been loaded with their mails, leave from the north or Henry Street gate.

The main operational work of the GPO fell to the Inland Office, which, under the oversight of a president and with some fifty staff, looked after the sorting, correct taxing and dispatch of Irish letters throughout the country. The staff here, who gradually worked their way up on the

---

4. House of Commons, *An Account of the Establishment of the General Post Office, in Ireland* (17 April 1822).

5. A money-order service had been operating in the Post Office since the late eighteenth century but, like the newspaper business, it was allowed to run as a private business operated by the GPO clerks.

basis of seniority, needed a firm grasp of geography and the senior men, the taxing clerks, were those responsible for applying the correct postage rate. This was calculated on the distance that each letter had to travel and it is important to remember that in this pre-postage-stamp era – the Penny Black arrived only in 1840 – the charge was generally paid by the recipient of the letter rather than the sender. A British Mail Office, which supervised the receipt and dispatch of mail to the sister island, maintained a separate but related existence to the Inland Office as did the curiously named Alphabet and Paid Window Office. The latter had two main functions. Firstly, it accepted money from the small minority of people who chose to pay their postage charges in advance to the clerk who worked at the paid window of the GPO. Secondly, it operated a form of private box-holder service – a type of *poste-restante* service – for letters addressed to other state departments like the Custom House and also for commercial correspondence addressed to merchants who, in return for paying an extra fee to have their mail abstracted and sorted to a pigeon-hole 'alphabet' frame, were allowed to call for it before the normal delivery had been dispatched. John Somers and James Hamilton, the two clerks who shared the duties of alphabet

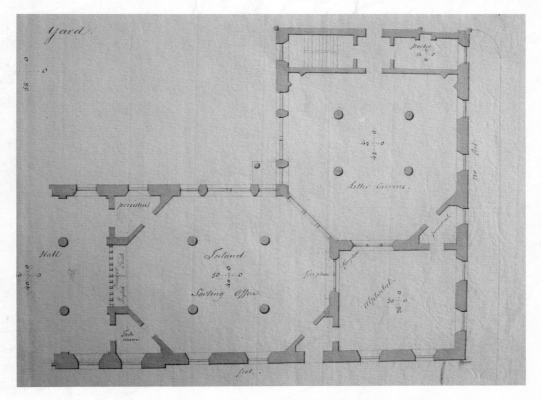

Johnston placed the main sorting office to the right of the GPO entrance hall, with letter boxes or 'receivers', which distinguished between English and Irish mail, provided for the public. (Courtesy of the Irish Architectural Archive)

keeper, had a heavy schedule: whichever was on duty had to be at his desk from 6.30 a.m. until at least 7 p.m. during the week, attend various public offices on Saturdays to assess their postage and put in two hours on Sunday to deal with mail that had arrived on the packet ship.

Once the letters had been sorted, they were ready for delivery by the letter carriers, of whom sixty were attached to the GPO. Of these, forty attended to the delivery of the Irish mails and twenty to the British mails. The city was divided into separate districts and each man had, as each postman still does, an assigned walk or route to be followed. Salaries varied from £68 16s. 0d. for first-class letter carriers like James Magee to the £36 8s. 0d. earned by Arundel Gore who was a lowly fifth-class man.[6] A little extra might be picked up by the men through bell-ringing fees – a penny per letter handed to them by members of the public – and gifts at Christmas time, but the wages were not high.

The GPO actually housed two complementary businesses and delivery staffs, the General Post and the Penny Post. The General Post, from which the building of course derives its name, was concerned with the transmission of letters, domestic and foreign, and stemmed from what had been the General Letter Office originally established by Charles II in 1660. The Penny Post Office was a later creation. One had been set up in London in 1680 and Dublin was the next city to have one, although that did not happen until 1773. This office handled letters that were to be delivered within the city boundaries and up to four miles beyond them. It was designed to provide a cheap and efficient delivery system for private and business correspondence within the capital, and mail was sorted and delivered by letter carriers who formed a distinct staff within the GPO. The idea proved popular and Penny Posts were gradually established in other towns throughout Ireland. The success of the system, which was cheap, frequent and efficient in comparison with the expensive general post, led in time to the introduction of Rowland Hill's universal Penny Post in 1840. While Hill's reforms made Penny Posts redundant, the introduction of the new rate did not lead immediately to the amalgamation of the two systems in the GPO. *The Post-Office Directory and Calendar* for 1844, for instance, lists a separate Penny Post Office network and details the five letter deliveries in Dublin, starting at 8 a.m. and finishing with a delivery at 8.30 p.m., but the second or noon delivery is still restricted to Penny Post correspondence.

The impact of universal penny postage on the lives of ordinary people in Britain and Ireland was profound but gradual, as older systems were not immediately replaced. People were not obliged to use the new postage stamps on their letters and they could choose to ignore

OPPOSITE: *Arthur O'Leary, the Tralee-born composer, capitalised on the growing interest in stamp collecting in* The Stamp Galop.

---

6. *Commissioners of Inquiry, Nineteenth Report*, p. 224

THE STAMP GALOP

Saxony.   Tuscany.   United States.   Australia.   France.   Hamburgh.   England.

India.   Naples.   Germany.   Prussia.   Germany.   Papal States.   Lubeck.

Switzerland.   Germany.   Victoria.   United States.   Italy.   Russia.   England.

French Repub.   India.   Naples.   Austria.   Brunswick.   Western Australia.   Oldenburgh.

Spain.   Prussia.   Belgium.   Greece.   India.   Hanover.   Denmark.

Bavaria.   Austria.   Italy.   England.   Switzerland.   Prussia.   Baden.

COMPOSED BY

ARTHUR O'LEARY.

ENT. STA. HALL.   PRICE 2/.

LONDON, EWER & Cº

PARIS, G. FLAXLAND 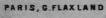 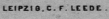 LEIPZIG, C. F. LEEDE.

inventions like letter boxes and continue to hand in their correspondence at their local post office. With his intimate knowledge of the Post Office, this is something Anthony Trollope portrays occasionally in his novels. He has, for instance, Miss Jemima Stanbury in *He Knew He Was Right* saying that she, for one:

> could not understand why people could not walk with their letters to a respectable post-office instead of chucking them into an iron stump ... out in the middle of the street.

Writing a letter, of course, would have been beyond the abilities of many people at this time, but as literacy improved so did the business of the Post Office. While the extraordinary industrialisation of the Victorian era affected only a small part of Ireland, the impact of population growth, of railway development and improvements in education meant that the GPO and its services grew in importance. With greater interest in its services came pressure for reform of its bureaucratic operations. The high cost of postage was singled out as a particular grievance. Postage rates throughout Ireland, for instance, had long been based on a cumbersome system that involved both distance and the number of sheets of paper in the letter. It was not only a complicated but also a very expensive postal service, and the costs were well beyond the pockets of ordinary people. The system involved the calculation by GPO clerks of a distinct rate for each letter and, generally speaking, the collection of the postage fee from the recipient of the letter rather than the person who posted it. While he was not initially in favour of a single uniform rate for letters, it gradually became Rowland Hill's belief that a standard flat rate, based on weight, would greatly simplify the service and increase Post Office revenue. Public dissatisfaction was soon reflected in parliament and culminated in the introduction of penny postage and the famous Penny Black stamp in 1840. Few stamps, perhaps, are as well known as it is. The classic profile of a young Queen Victoria on a small square of black paper is recognisable to people who never swopped a stamp in their lives and for whom the name of the world's most famous stamp dealer, Stanley Gibbons, provokes merely a shrug of incomprehension.

It is justly famous, of course, as the world's first postage stamp, but its creation – in terms of its effect on education and literacy for instance – had an influence that went far beyond the immediate benefit of simplified accounting, which it brought to the GPO's accounting clerks. The invention of a little gummed label, which might be stuck to an envelope to signify that

OPPOSITE: *Although he had been obliged to leave Dublin's GPO, Sir Edward Lees remained an important figure in the Post Office, and this circular on the introduction of the new postage labels was issued from Edinburgh under his name.* (Courtesy of the National Museum of Ireland)

TO ALL POSTMASTERS.

GENERAL POST OFFICE,
Edinburgh, April, 1840.

I BEG to inclose you two Specimens of the Penny and Two-penny stamped Covers and Envelopes, and two of the Penny adhesive Labels, (the Two-penny one is not yet ready) which I must beg you will carefully preserve, in order to compare them in case of doubt with the stamped Letters that may pass through your Office. In the event of your suspecting that the Stamps used on any Letters are forged, you will not detain the Letter, but simply take the Address, and report the circumstance to me without loss of time, in order that the Party to whom the Letter is directed may be at once applied to. You will observe, however, that the adhesive Stamps vary almost in all cases, one from the other, having different Letters at the bottom corners, and I point this out that you may not be misled by the circumstance, and be induced to suspect Forgery, where the variation of the Stamps has been intentional. The Numbers on the Covers and Envelopes also vary. You will carefully Stamp with the Cancelling Stamp that has been forwarded to you, the stamped Covers and Envelopes, as well as the adhesive Stamps, the two former must be struck on the figure of Britannia, and in case of more than one adhesive Stamp being attached to a Letter, each Stamp must be separately obliterated. The use of the Cancelling Stamp, however, will not dispense with that of the ordinary dated Stamp, which will be struck on the Letter as usual. Where the value of the Stamps is under the rate of Postage, to which the Letter if pre-paid in Money would be subject, you will Surcharge the Letter with a Pen in the usual manner.

You will acknowledge the receipt of this Letter and the Specimen Stamps by return of Post.

By Command,

EDWARD S. LEES,

SECRETARY.

An object of desire for generations of stamp collectors, the Penny Black, with its profile of a young Queen Victoria, set a very high standard for stamp design and production.

payment for postage had been made, is credited to Rowland Hill, the dominant figure of the nineteenth-century British Post Office, but there were others who played their part too, among whom were Augustus Godby, who followed Lees as secretary of the GPO in Dublin. In 1839, as part of an open Treasury competition to come up with a design for what would become the world's first postage stamp, he submitted to London a pen and ink sketch of his own. It was a simple affair, more a folded letter or envelope than a postage stamp, and it is sealed with what must have been his own motto: 'Not words but deeds'. It was a suitable motto for the man in charge of the GPO because his staff there would have had to work hard to cope with the huge increase in mail volumes caused by the Penny Black and cheap postage; the number of letters almost doubled from 9,356,412 in 1839 to 18,210,642 in 1840.

The story associated with just one of those letters is of special interest to the historian of the GPO, for when this particular letter came up for auction in Dublin a few years ago, it generated much interest in philatelic circles having been posted in Dublin on 8 May 1840, just a few days after the new Penny Black labels were put on sale. Research into the letter and the family of the author added to its interest, revealing a story of youthful expectation and hints of unfulfilled romance that linked rural Cavan with India's North-Western Provinces. Its author, Frederick Fitzpatrick, was a clergyman from Shercock in County Cavan who, having just arrived back from England on the boat with his son, sat down in the Londonderry Hotel at 5 Bolton Street, Dublin (the site now occupied by the Dublin Institute of Technology), to write to his friend and solicitor in London. It's a short letter, hard to decipher and would be of little interest but for the good fortune that a collection of correspondence from the same family survives in the collection of Trinity College Library. Studying these letters suggests an answer to a puzzling question that immediately arises in the case of the Rev. Fitzpatrick's letter, namely, where did he buy his Penny Black stamps? Although it seems that a supply of the stamps had been dispatched to Dublin from London on 4 May, these would have been sent to the Stamp Office in the Custom House in the first instance rather than to the GPO, and it is most unlikely that any were on sale so soon in Dublin. The Trinity College Library correspondence, however, makes it clear that the Fitzpatricks were diligent letter writers and kept in touch through the post. Joseph Fitzpatrick, Frederick's son, was

The Fitzpatrick-Thomas letter of 8 May 1840 is of considerable philatelic interest as it marks the first unambiguous usage of the Penny Black in Ireland.

at school in England and, writing to his mother from Haileybury in Hertfordshire on 25 January 1840, readily expresses the important place of the post in their lives.

> I arrived here all right last evening and this morning got your letter with great gladness ... Did you get a letter from me from Liverpool?

Just at the end of his letter home, Joseph adds these very significant words: 'No stamps out yet'.[7] It is only a passing reference but sufficient for us to glean that the Fitzpatricks had been keenly following the course of the postal reform debates and were keeping their eyes peeled for the much anticipated new postage labels, eager, presumably, to use them on their letters. It would seem, from this reference, that the mystery of how Penny Blacks appeared on a Dublin letter on 8 May 1840, at a time when it is most unlikely they were on sale anywhere in the city, is best explained by the fact that they were acquired in England, probably London, by Frederick Fitzpatrick. He must have been glad of the chance to use them on his letter to Lincoln's Inn Fields in London and, with no street letter boxes in place at the time, he probably walked the short distance to the GPO, proud of the fact that he was an early adopter of this innovation!

---

7. Trinity College Dublin (TCD), *Fitzpatrick correspondence*, Ms. 2318/1–6.

As the Post Office grew, so did the desire of staff to unite in pursuit of better pay and conditions. This attractive New Year's card was produced by the Dublin Postmen's Federation.

Perhaps he even stopped for a chat with the GPO clerks and showed them his letter. No doubt it caused, with its newfangled stamps, a bit of discussion among the staff on duty as they applied an afternoon date stamp and put it in the bag for the early-evening dispatch to Liverpool.

The introduction of cheap postage and the stamps that accompanied this reform transformed the work of the Post Office and gradually made the GPO a recognised and popular manifestation of government. As the department expanded its business into areas like savings banks, insurance and annuities, telegraphs and finally telephones in the early twentieth century, the critical importance of the GPO to the social and economic well-being not only of Dublin but of the whole of Ireland was unquestionable. The extension of Post Office services to include parcel delivery in 1883 was an important step in the development of the business and had the immediate effect of changing the old title of letter carrier to postman. The older name, however, lives on in the United States in the title of one postal union, the National Association of Letter Carriers. All sorts of things, including living creatures, were sent through the parcel post, and a live snake, which had escaped from a package on the mail boat between Holyhead and Dublin, was donated to Dublin Zoo. Some time later a pair of live lizards were found in the GPO in a parcel from the USA but, in this instance, the animals were claimed before contact was made with the zookeepers in the Phoenix Park.

Expansion in the scale and range of its operations naturally put pressure on space in the GPO, and with each new development and the need to accommodate new equipment or more staff, there was a corresponding alteration in the internal layout of the building, with a room divided here and a wall knocked down there. This naturally did some injury to Johnston's original design which had been conceived for an organisation that was focused almost exclusively on the collection, sorting and delivery of letters. The postal system with which he was familiar occupied itself in tasks that had not changed much in two centuries: mail volumes were small as was the staff, and while he had seen the successful introduction of the mail-coach and had incorporated its daily use into his architectural plans, he could not have envisaged the vast increase in the scale and scope of Post Office activity in the fifty years after his death. The constant tinkering with the internal fabric gave way to a more thorough remodelling of the building in 1870–71. In his report to the Treasury, William Monsell, Liberal MP for County Limerick and postmaster general in William Ewart Gladstone's government, announced that:

> At the General Post Office in Dublin a new and spacious office has been opened in which Post Office business, instead of being any longer distributed among several rooms in different parts of the building, is brought together in one room and transacted across an open counter.[8]

Having an Irishman at Westminster as postmaster general may have encouraged other improvements such as the establishment of various Dublin suburban post offices and the addition of a sixth daily delivery from the GPO 'to take place at half past three in the afternoon as the hour most convenient for business purposes'.

The renovations of 1870–71 must have been due, in part, to the need to accommodate the technical equipment and additional staff that joined the Post Office when it took over private telegraph companies on 5 February 1870. The transfer of this work from the private sector to the Post Office was an important development and represented a new challenge for the department. That it took a little time to get used to things is clear from the fact that the Dublin Chamber of Commerce passed in 1870 a resolution condemning the manner in which the Post Office was conducting the telegraph business and calling for redress. The advent of the telegraph work was highly significant for the GPO for two reasons: not only did it introduce a new and highly technical element to the work of the Post Office but it also introduced women to the workforce. Until then women had worked in the GPO only as domestic staff, but because the telegraph companies had employed them as telegraphists, they came as part of the nationalisation package. Women made up just under a quarter of the telegraph department's staff, which was a big change for the GPO. They did not do any night work and were paid from 12s. to 20s. per week, their male colleagues earning 14s. to £2. *The Freeman's Journal* acknowledged that

---

8. Her Majesty's Stationery Office (HMSO), *Seventeenth Report of the Postmaster General on The Post Office*, p. 13.

How charming! Shall we accept?

The telephone business was taken over by the Post Office in 1912, and the telephone gradually became an essential tool of business and a desirable gadget for the aspiring socialite.

the girls did pick up the skills quicker than the boys, but in an interesting defence of the pay differential, added:

> her quickness is purely digital, for her ignorance of public affairs, which a boy mends in some sort, militates against the progress she might otherwise make.

When a telegraph was received in the GPO's Instrument Room, it was written out and delivered by one of the telegraph boys, 'that little army of martyrs who are to be found careering in gleefullest humour through every street in the city'.[9]

While the editor of *The Irish Builder* was pleased with the various developments in postal technology and efficiency at the GPO, he was very critical of the renovations that had taken place then and in preceding years. The blocking up of the central arcade under the portico, which had led to the courtyard at the rear, had been carried out some time earlier, but the closing of all the chief central entrances that had led off the central hall contributed to what he saw as 'the shameful disfigurement of the building as an architectural feature in our metropolis' and a profound disservice to an architect who 'deserved better at the hands of the city he honoured'. The next move that might be expected, he continued, would be 'the removal of the columns and pediment in front of our General Post-office'. Warming to his theme, he adds that Johnston's portico 'stands now a dumb show, a refuge for pigeons above, and a refuge for sinners and the rain and storm-driven below.' To his mind, the GPO officials had ignored the potential of the space in the yard at the rear of the building and had pressed ahead with their 'darling schemes of centralisation and postal economy' in a development 'much akin to vandalism'.[10]

The removal of the principal entrance from the front of the GPO and subsequent creation instead of an entrance around the corner in Prince's Street certainly did nothing for Johnston's design and gave rise to the Dublin jibe about the GPO being the only building in Sackville Street without a front door. The railings on the Prince's Street side of the building were removed in 1871 and the pavement widened a little. The extra space provided to the citizens of Dublin prompted the Lord Mayor and Sir John Gray, among others, to see if the matter might be pressed in relation to Henry Street as well and the postmaster general was reported to be glad that he could 'without detriment to the service, accede to the request made on behalf of the citizens of Dublin'.[11] New post boxes, marked 'English' and 'Foreign' and lettered in red and black, were installed under the GPO portico, but the editor of *The Irish Builder* was not

---

9. *The Freeman's Journal*, quoted in *The Irish Builder* (15 September 1871).
10. *The Irish Builder* (1871) vol. 13, no. 282, p. 237.
11. *The Freeman's Journal* (17 April 1871).

happy with the lighting provided for the public, who 'had to grope out the proper slits, unless,' as he lyrically expresses it, 'the autumnal moon is in one of her indulgent moods'.[12]

It seems there was also some consideration given at this time to expansion of the GPO through the acquisition of the Ball's Bank premises in Henry Street but, in the event, this did not happen until a generation later. Piecemeal work continued on aspects of the building and related premises as occasion demanded, with alterations to the stables maintained at 86 Marlborough Street executed for an estimated £50 and a new glass shed to shelter the mail vans in the GPO built for a provision of £992.[13] The living accommodation and ancillary space, which had been provided for various members of staff under Johnston's plan, was reduced in favour of the expanding business of the GPO, but there were still a few people for whom the GPO provided a home, notably the caretaker and his family. One man who filled this position was William Lawrence who came to the GPO from Wales as labourer-in-trust in 1831 and is named in later directories as clerk of works. His accommodation in the building provided a view of the back yard and family papers recall that he would 'watch the Royal Mail Coaches leave the back yard of the GPO with drivers in red livery and brass trumpets' as they set off for Cork, Waterford, Galway and Belfast. This William was the father of William Mervin Lawrence, who was born in the GPO on 5 July 1840 and is remembered today as the man behind the National Library's wonderful collection of Irish photographs. William's daughter, Rebecca, holds what must be the unique distinction of being the only woman to have been married from the GPO. She was married on 2 April 1857 and in the marriage register of the old St Thomas' church, just a stone's throw from the door of the GPO, her residence is recorded as the General Post Office.[14] William Lawrence retired to Blackrock and died in 1887 in his ninetieth year. He and his wife Elizabeth are buried in Dean's Grange Cemetery, where the tombstone proudly describes him as 'Late of General Post Office Dublin'.

As the century passed, change was to be found not only in the scope and extent of the GPO's business but also in its own recruitment and promotion polices. The old system, based very much on family contacts, recommendations and connections, was not suited to running what was in effect a vast government business. The Victorians came to believe that a strict adherence to codified rules and procedures could bring benefits to the civil service in much the same way as Dickens' characters Thomas Gradgrind and Josiah Bounderby applied facts and discipline to education and industry. In particular, the recruitment of people to civil service departments was subject to success in open competitive examinations and not based on preferment, patronage or purchase. The new thinking was the result of an investigation, commissioned by Gladstone, into the

---

12. *The Irish Builder* (1871) vol. 13, no. 284, p. 266.

13. *Estimates for Civil Service for year ending 31st March 1875*, An Post archives.

14. The GPO is remarkable for the fact that a parish boundary runs through the middle of the building, the front portion being in St Thomas' while the rear belongs to St Mary's parish.

William Lawrence, GPO clerk of works and progenitor of the famous Dublin photographic family. (Private collection)

The circulation of the mails was the preoccupation of the GPO's surveyors, who regularly plotted and revised the intricate network of rail, coach and foot connections throughout Ireland.

operation and organisation of the civil service, of which the Post Office formed a considerable part. Sir Stafford Northcote and Charles Trevelyan, both senior figures in the civil service, undertook the work, and their report, published in February 1854, became the foundation for a particular view of the civil service as politically impartial and educationally generalist, with entry and promotion based on merit assessed by competition. Its influence, though diminished, can still be found today, and the values it espoused – integrity, objectivity and an apolitical outlook – retain their appeal. For people like Trollope, who had been recruited to the GPO on the basis of a family connection, and had risen through the ranks by means of application and practical experience, the idea of competitive examinations and regular transfer between civil service departments made little sense. He wrote an article, published in the *Dublin University Magazine* in October 1855, criticising proposals that required academic accomplishments likely to be far beyond what would be needed to do most civil service jobs and arguing instead for the advantages of practical training that came with doing the job. It is an argument that has always had particular relevance for staff of the GPO, where the application of strict seniority rules has strongly influenced advancement.

In 1871 the GPO employed 606 staff, about half of whom worked in the sorting office. A large contingent of boys would wait inside the office for the letters to be posted through the letter boxes, or 'receivers' as they are technically known, and then arrange them face up ready to be obliterated with the date stamp.[15] Primary sorting into broad divisions followed and then further distribution into minor divisions, with sorting into individual 'walks' the last task undertaken by the relevant postmen. One newspaper reporter was duly impressed:

> Every hole you can see has the name of a place or a district printed over it; but the sorters are so skilful that they never raise their eyes from the address but just launch the letter to its place.[16]

Organisational efficiency won the respect of the public, who came to expect a very high standard of service. When a letter went astray or was damaged, the complaint was treated seriously, with a reply often signed by the secretary himself. This one, sent in 1874 from the secretary, G. C. Cornwall, to a Mr Henry Toal of Moy, County Tyrone, who was concerned about possible interference with his letter, is characteristic of the customer service of the time:

> Sir, In reply to your letter of the 18th instant, I beg to inform you that the matter has been fully enquired into, but nothing has been elicited to show that the letter in question was tampered with,

---

15. The rather frightening term 'obliteration' refers to the process of cancelling the stamp in the post office. In 1844 a system of numbered obliterations was introduced throughout Great Britain and Ireland, with Dublin being assigned 186 in the Irish series.

16. *The Freeman's Journal*, quoted in *The Irish Builder* (15 September 1871).

whilst in the custody of the Department. It is presumed from the inferior quality of the paper which the envelope is composed of, that the fracture was accidental and arose from pressure in the mail bag.

Indeed, in his report for that year, the postmaster general drew attention to those who sometimes made groundless charges against the Post Office and while the institution did not 'for one moment claim to be immaculate' he was sure that his department would be supported by public opinion against those who pronounced judgement 'on a mere indictment which is unsupported by evidence'.[17] These words might well have been pondered a decade or so later when the same Gustavus Cornwall who had drawn attention to the inferior quality of Mr Toal's envelope found himself very much on the wrong side of public opinion.

The confluence of personal and public matters within the broad context of the GPO, which had eventually forced the removal of one secretary, Sir Edward Lees, in 1831, came to the fore again in 1884 in the case of Cornwall. He was a career Post Office man who had risen to be secretary of the Irish Post Office when he was overtaken in his twilight years by a political storm that brought into question his personal morality. The later Victorians, of course, maintained a standard of respectability and behaviour that allowed little leeway for those who were unwilling or unable to conform to the exacting demands of polite society. Homosexuality was privately acknowledged within the higher ranks of society but it was a criminal offence and practising homosexuals were obliged to live a life of rather sordid secrecy. The Christianity of the period had resurrected and applied in some measure to its own time the ideals of the medieval knight, of men who were pure, dutiful to God and chivalrous to women, men who were certain of their place and knew how to administer civil service departments and enormous swathes of empire. When Cornwall's name was mentioned in an article published by William O'Brien, editor of the nationalist paper *United Ireland*, accusing prominent figures within the Irish administration in Dublin Castle of unnatural practices, Cornwall, then sixty-two years old, took a libel case against the publication. A stern man with a commanding presence, he must, nonetheless, have felt himself facing a challenge beyond anything he had seen in the comparatively tranquil corridors of Dublin's GPO. He lost his libel case in July 1884 and was suspended from his position in the GPO. Over the following year, the *affaire* – which was essentially a political attack from nationalist quarters on the Lord Lieutenant, Earl Spencer – rolled on, with Cornwall acquitted of the various charges brought against him. He then made an attempt to appeal the original decision in the libel case but ran out of money. Even though he was acquitted, he was obliged to resign in August 1885, and despite his forty-five years of Post Office service he was denied a pension. It was a sad end for a man who had been a respected civil servant, but it was also a

17. HMSO, *Twentieth Report of the Postmaster General on the Post Office* (1864), p. 9.

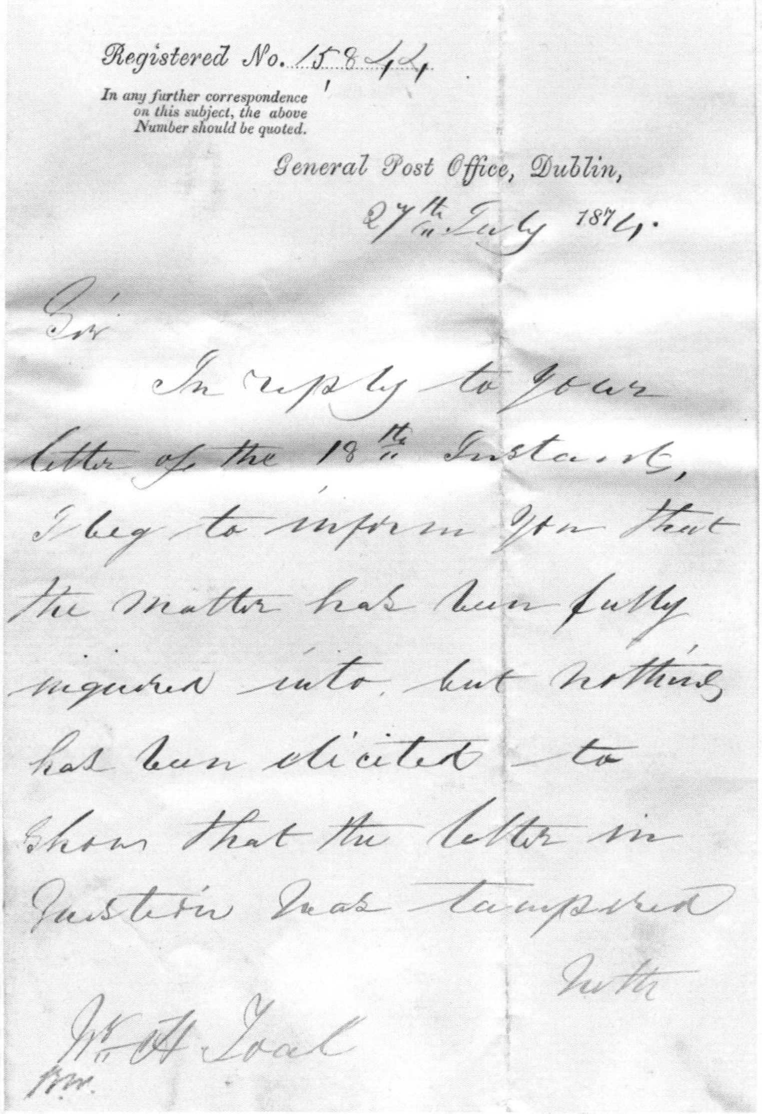

Registered No. 15844.

In any further correspondence
on this subject, the above
Number should be quoted.

General Post Office, Dublin,

27th July 1874.

Sir,

In reply to your
letter of the 18th Instant,
I beg to inform You that
the matter has been fully
inquired into, but nothing
has been elicited to
show that the letter in
question was tampered
with

Wm. H. Ical
Wm.

The quality of its service was a matter of pride for GPO officials, and replies to complaints, such as this 1874 letter signed by the secretary, G. C. Cornwall, were promptly issued.

OVERLEAF: This 1887 Christmas card from the GPO's sorting office staff highlights that their work also embraced daily rail and ship sorting. (Private collection)

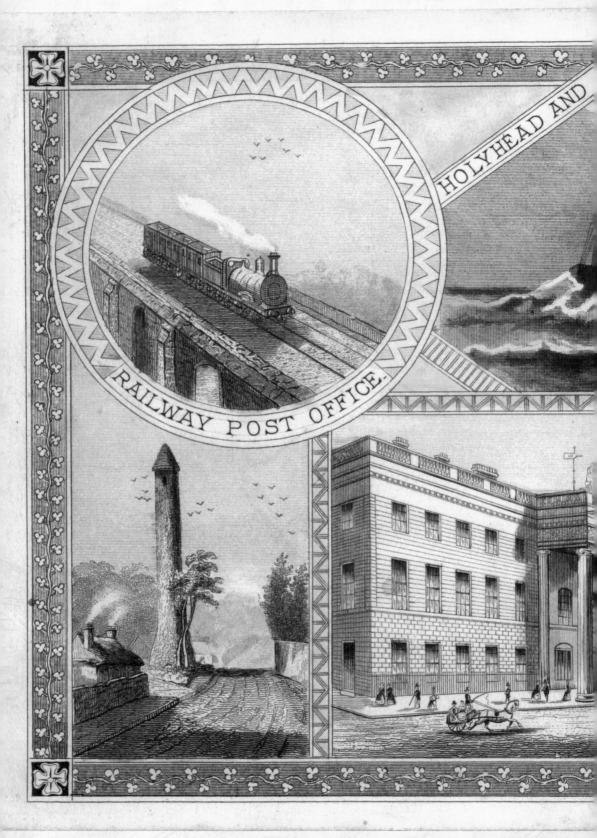

RAILWAY POST OFFICE.

HOLYHEAD AND

clear signal that the Post Office, as a business, was not prepared to run the risk of tarnishing the reputation for respectability it had won in the course of Queen Victoria's reign.

By the end of the century the scale and scope of GPO business would have amazed those who worked in the building back in the 1820s. The development of the institution into the greatest revenue-producing department of the state with a presence in even the remotest parts of the country would have astonished them, for they could not have anticipated the profound influence wrought by the introduction of the Penny Black, the railway and the telegraph. Their GPO, though housed in a beautiful new building that brought classical elegance to Sackville Street, was essentially an eighteenth-century organisation founded on patronage and the benefits that might be extracted from a political system that generally placed loyalty and family connections above hard work and ability. A remarkable transformation, in terms of technological innovation and operational efficiency, had been achieved and the GPO presided over an organisation which had unparalleled influence in Ireland. The introduction of old-age pensions by the government in 1909 and their payment through post offices not only reinforced this dominant position, but also cemented a close relationship between local post offices, as the agents and representatives of the GPO and Dublin government in general, and the often isolated rural communities they served. The GPO's senior staff who sat down in the restaurant of the neighbouring Metropole Hotel in 1898 – the first occasion on which an annual social dinner was held – had a right to feel pleased with themselves. While volumes per head of population continued, in most mail categories, to be lower than those for England and Scotland, the Post Office was intimately connected with the daily affairs of ordinary people in Ireland in a way that could not have been imagined a century earlier. Within the next year the postmaster general, Lord Londonderry, would be able to present in his report for the year 1899–1900 a picture of a Post Office that, on the cusp of a new century, was, as table 1 indicates, at the very heart of social and business life in Ireland.

TABLE 1 – IRISH POST OFFICE BUSINESS VOLUMES IN 1900

Letters delivered	141,100,00
Post cards delivered	16,900,000
Books and circulars delivered	32,500,000
Newspapers delivered	19,100,000
Parcels delivered	4,860,000
Money orders delivered	588,885
Telegrams forwarded	4,910,939
Number of post offices	2,996
Number of staff	17,454

Toasts to the queen, the postmaster general, the secretary and the former secretary, who had come back specially from his post in Edinburgh to join his former colleagues, were proposed. Social change, political turmoil and war were not yet on the horizon and the conversation might have ranged happily from the most suitable uniforms for potential women 'postmen' to the old chestnut of the need for more space in the GPO.

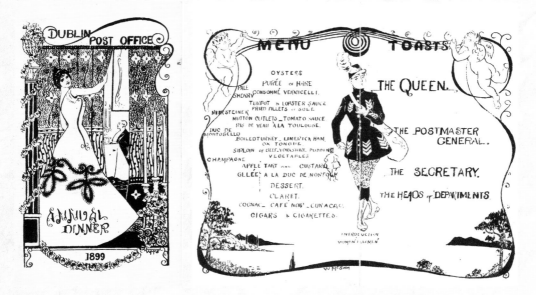

This attractive art-nouveau-style menu, produced for the annual GPO dinner, dates from 1899.

By the closing decades of the nineteenth century the enormous growth in the size and scope of Post Office business meant that the GPO was bursting at the seams. The ordered purpose of the original design had been subsumed into a haphazard and confused maze of rooms and corridors quite inadequate for staff and public alike. The weight of the GPO bells had begun to pose a danger and they were taken down in 1881. A few years later, in 1888, Andrew Robinson, who was assistant surveyor of the Commissioners of Public Works, examined the building and managed successfully to underpin its structure. There was general agreement both within the GPO and in the wider public mind that facilities were below standard. R. A. Egerton, Dublin secretary, writing on 18 September 1906 to his boss in London, reported, 'The Public Office is lamentably behind the times.'[18] Suitable space for the public was lacking, while working arrangements for staff were quite inadequate, with congestion a common complaint especially during the dispatch of the night mails and during the tourist season. Sorting work was carried on in full view of the

---

18. NAI TEC/197406/7.

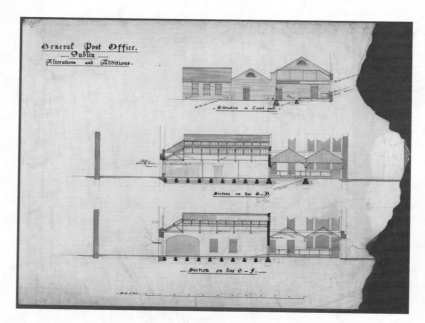

Finding space to accommodate the expanding workload at the GPO was a constant problem, and this elevation of c. 1883 shows a building to be erected within the former coach yard. (Courtesy of the National Archives of Ireland)

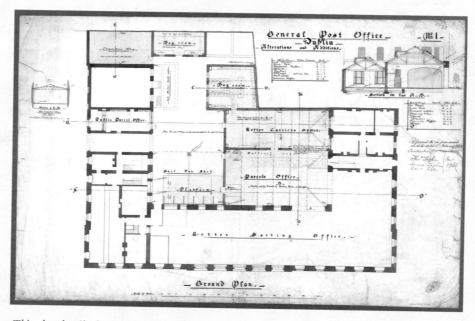

This plan details the operational layout that existed before Pentland's work on the creation of a new public office in the space occupied by the main letter-sorting office, which takes up almost the entire width of the GPO's ground floor. (Courtesy of the National Archives of Ireland)

posting public, who might well have appreciated this glimpse of the GPO's staff at work. To the secretary and his staff it was a cause of dismay and represented a security risk and an affront to the department's self-respect.

One curious matter that remains puzzling and that did not emerge until recent years is tied up with this lack of space in the GPO and its reputation, perhaps, as a warren of corridors and hidden cubbyholes. This is the alleged discovery of a hoard of very valuable old stamps during renovation work in the GPO in the closing years of the nineteenth century. A file in the Post Office archive in London entitled 'Old stamps found in Dublin' and the recollections of some important figures in the stamp world of that period indicate that, in some forgotten cupboard in the GPO, unused sheets of Penny Blacks and similar material were unearthed. This gave rise to questions as to how — at a time of very keen interest in the hobby — this treasure should be treated. Closer investigation into the story suggests, however, that the Dublin GPO may have been used as a convenient provincial 'source' for stamps that had in fact been found in London and were to be sold surreptitiously at a huge profit, for the benefit of the Treasury.[19]

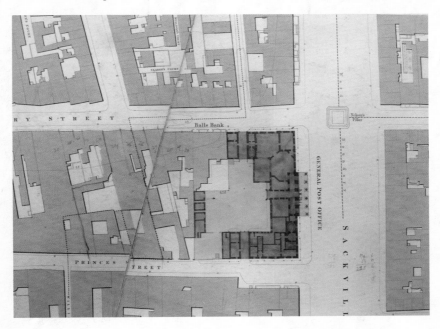

While the outline of Johnston's design can still be seen in this Ordnance Survey plan of 1864, it is clear that there has been encroachment on the entrance hall, which is narrower. The passage through to the yard will remain until the 1870–71 remodelling of the sorting office. Note, too, the Ball's Bank premises, which will eventually be purchased by the GPO in 1906. (Courtesy of the Office of Public Works)

19. The story of the 'discovery' and subsequent fate of these stamps is told in *The Dublin Find* by Don Madden and Karl Louis.

The ranks of letter boxes under the portico can just be seen in this colour-tinted view of the GPO.

Mr. Robert Cochrane, LL.D., I.S.O.

Robert Cochrane and Howard Pentland, Board of Works architects, were responsible for the major extension and renovation works undertaken in the early years of the twentieth century.
(Courtesy of the Irish Architectural Archive)

Unremitting pressure on space led eventually to the purchase of Ball's Bank (subsequently incorporated into the Northern Bank) in Henry Street by the Post Office in 1903 at a cost of £12,000. The remodelling of this building was the first phase of an ambitious three-phase expansion and renovation of the GPO that would be gradually carried out over the next dozen years and be completed only a few weeks before the total destruction of the building in 1916. It was carried out by the architects of the Board of Works under the direction of the two principal architects, Robert Cochrane and Howard Pentland. Cochrane was a County Down man, educated at Queen's in Belfast, who joined the Board of Works in 1874. An antiquarian as well as an architect, he served as president of the Royal Society of Antiquaries and also held the post of inspector of ancient monuments, for which he was eminently suited. His obituary in *The Irish Builder* of 25 March 1916 calls him 'one of the most striking and forceful personalities of the architectural profession in Ireland', a man who 'never aspired to brilliancy' but whose work was distinguished by 'absolute thoroughness'. He designed a number of post office buildings throughout Ireland as well as being responsible for the Ball's Bank phase of the GPO extension and the initial stages of work on the Prince's Street wing, which was completed by J. H. Pentland.

The banking hall lent itself to relatively straightforward adaptation for postal purposes and was occupied by sorting-office administrative staff – the controller, chief clerk, superintendents and thirty clerks – who dealt with general correspondence, establishment and survey work. This work was completed by 1906 and removed some of the immediate pressure on space in the GPO, but the acquisition of the bank was just part of the much larger redevelopment plan and did not of itself lead to the significant increase in general working and administrative space that was required.

Proposals outlined in a draft letter to the Treasury on 1 August 1906 set out the more extensive plan, which envisaged building on ground known as Findlater's and Lalouette's yards on the Prince's Street side of the GPO. The proposed extension work was estimated to cost some £18,000, but the costing details and the potential for expansion of services were the subject of much politely phrased but seriously argued correspondence between GPO officials in Dublin and the Treasury mandarins in London who believed that the money spent on the Ball's Bank extension ought to have provided sufficient new space. The matter was eventually settled to Dublin's satisfaction, helped perhaps by a visit of the postmaster general, Sydney Buxton, to Ireland. While in Dublin he had been 'shocked at the existing state of things' at the GPO and wanted 'to get all put straight and in good order as soon as possible'.[20] The plan proposed was the erection of an entirely new wing which would accommodate a new sorting office for the postmen, an improved registry for the secretary's office and new kitchen, dining and lavatory facilities. The medical officer, who saw an average of fifty staff each day, would be given more space, and the Telegraph Messengers' Institute, which provided educational and recreational facilities for the telegraph boys and was based in the College Green branch office, would be brought into the GPO too. In addition it was felt that there would be space under the new arrangement to bring the solicitor and his staff closer to the seat of power in the GPO and move them from their quarters at 14 Upper Sackville Street.

Dilapidated buildings on the site were cleared, as were former workshops at the rear of the GPO. Space for new workshops, which would accommodate Board of Works workmen, was found at Aldborough House, headquarters of the Post Office's stores department. The construction of this major work was supervised by Howard Pentland, who joined the Board of Works in 1884 after a spell in the office of T. N. Deane. Born in Lurgan and educated at Trinity, Pentland was a scholarly man with interests in languages and art and he brought a good understanding of steel and contemporary construction engineering to his work on the GPO. The Prince's Street wing comprised a three-storey-over-basement development, designed to be fireproof, with the floors formed of tubular concrete on cased-steel girders, supported by

---

20. NAI, TEC/197406/7.

cased-steel stanchions. The walls were chiefly brick, with the Prince's Street elevation faced with granite ashlar to match Johnston's finish on the original building. Completed in 1912, this extension added over 21,000 sq ft to the GPO's floor space.

This photograph of the new GPO public office, complete with Burmese-teak counters and Tuscan columns, was taken shortly before the destruction of 1916.

Pentland also supervised work on the final phase of the GPO renovation, the creation of a new public office. It was executed by the firm of J. and W. Stewart of Dublin and Belfast and involved the creation of an imposing segmental ceiling that spanned 40 ft and was supported by four Tuscan columns and two pilasters at each end. The entrance doorway was reinstated in the original block under Johnston's hexastyle portico, to the satisfaction, one hopes, of *The Irish Builder* editor who had quite rightly decried the vandalism of its closure forty years earlier. Long-standing critics of the cramped and dingy public office were now, at last, silenced by the creation of a spacious, light-filled public area, fitted out with Burmese-teak counters, a modern telephone 'silence cabinet' bearing a clock, and vitreous mosaic floors of a geometric pattern in harmony with Johnston's original conception. With the work finally completed in March 1916 – the same month that saw the death of Robert Cochrane – the various builders, architects, staff and customers were able to breathe a sigh of satisfaction. Little did they know that their time to appreciate this handsome addition to Dublin's architecture would be limited to just a few weeks.

Rebellion

❧ ❦

*Just then Desmond FitzGerald came out of a room and greeted me
affectionately, calling out, 'Hello, Claire' ... He asked me would I
have a cup of tea.*

Claire Hobson's memory of visiting the GPO
on Easter Monday

❧ ❦

For many Irish people, the response to the acronym GPO is immediate,
instinctive and emotional. The association, particularly perhaps for
younger people, who communicate more by texting and tweeting than
by letter, is not so much with the organisation that delivers post and pays
pensions but with the building where the Easter Rising began in 1916;
the connection with the postal service takes an extra second or two to
strike the mind. As our country prepares to mark the centenary of that
event, many historians, through the study of new evidence and accounts
that continue to emerge, are hoping to open up fresh perspectives on a
week that left a legacy of division as well as a fire of inspiration.

The passage of time may well make it impossible to be certain
exactly what men did and why they did it but it has the great advantage
of allowing passions to cool and discussion to take place. With great
and far-reaching events like the American and French Revolutions,
World War I and, within a more modest framework, our own 1916
story, it takes a long time before a fair understanding can emerge.
Politics and mythology, resentment and stubbornness can distort our

A Lawrence view of the GPO taken at a time when the trams were still horse-drawn and the lamps had been removed from their lamp stands outside the GPO portico. (National Library of Ireland)

capacity to appreciate the complexity of private motivation and public utterance, and there is certainly some truth in G. M. Trevelyan's remark that 'Some nations, like the Irish, are *too* historically minded, in the sense that they cannot get out of the past at all.'[1] One of the privileges of working in the GPO over many years has been the opportunity occasionally to meet the descendants of people who took part in the rebellion. The memories and stories passed down to them reflect, to a great extent, the broad range of aspirations, qualities and emotions that possessed the small band of men and women who occupied the GPO during Easter Week. Most were young, and idealism – whether around Irish independence, a fairer society or the rights of women – was the driving force that inspired them. There were also those whose spirits lit up simply by being part of an adventure, and a few bold souls joined the GPO garrison without any previous connection whatever with the nationalist movement. Michael Cremen, a clerk in the Post Office's stores department in Aldborough House, remembered seeing a man on the roof of

1.   Trevelyan, G. M., *An Autobiography & Other Essays* (Longmans, Green & Co., London, 1949), p. 63.

Issued for the anniversary of Pearse's birth, Robert Ballagh's stamp design draws on Delacroix's painting of Liberty Leading the People. *James Connolly looks relaxed in the photograph used for this anniversary stamp issued in 1968.*

the GPO who didn't seem to be part of any group or unit he had come across. When he asked him who he was, the man confessed he had been a bystander in Sackville Street and, hearing Connolly looking for volunteers, decided to join the rebellion there and then.[2]

2. Bureau of Military History (BMH) WS 563.

Of course idealism and a sense of adventure, coupled with the need to find employment, had inspired many young Irish men, from Belfast to Bandon, to join the British Army and fight in Flanders or Gallipoli. Home Rule had been promised and who knows what would have happened if the GPO's clerks had gone home undisturbed that Easter Monday and the Proclamation been left unprinted? Speculating on the might-have-beens of history is fun but in the end fruitless, and we must return to the young Desmond FitzGerald and his cheery offer of a cup of tea to Bulmer Hobson's wife on that pleasant spring day in Dublin nearly a hundred years ago.

A letter addressed to Thomas Clarke, one of the signatories of the Proclamation. It bears a Sinn Féin propaganda label and an ordinary stamp, inverted as a sign of disrespect to the King.

A few hours before FitzGerald had been put in charge of catering arrangements in the rebel headquarters, A. H. Norway, secretary of the Irish Post Office, had dropped in briefly to his room on the first floor. It was a bank holiday and outside the GPO in Sackville Street people strolled, enjoying the welcome warmth and the relaxed atmosphere in town. Inside the Post Office a reduced staff was on duty keeping essential services open to the public. At about 11.45 a.m. Norway was summoned by telephone to Dublin Castle. On his way to that meeting, he might, had he glanced down Lower Abbey Street towards the old Liberty Hall, have seen a group of people assembling in an ordered and purposeful fashion. Had he loitered a few minutes longer, he would have seen that group march up the street towards him, wheel right into Sackville Street and suddenly break ranks outside the GPO and charge into the very building he had just left. By that time, however, he would have been entering the Castle to be informed that the government suspected a rebellion might well be imminent.

Unlike many who had tried before them, Patrick Pearse and James Connolly, who were at the head of the band that entered the Post Office, had managed to maintain the secrecy of their plans for an armed rebellion. It was maintained, however, at the cost of some confusion, as a notice cancelling the manoeuvres planned for the Irish Volunteers on Easter Sunday appeared in that morning's paper. This was the work of Eoin MacNeill, head of the Irish Volunteers, who realised just a few days before the Rising that he had been deliberately misled by Pearse and an inner circle of Irish Republican Brotherhood (IRB) members about their true intentions. He initially resigned himself to the inevitability of a rebellion but confirmation of the sinking of the German arms ship, *Aud*, and the arrest of Sir Roger Casement in Kerry led to his circulation of a note declaring that the Volunteers had been 'completely deceived' and cancelling all arrangements for Easter Sunday.

BELOW: *Broken windows and the clock on the wall of the GPO yard.* (Courtesy of Mercier Press Archive)

When Pearse and the other leaders met in Liberty Hall on Easter Sunday morning their resolve remained unshakeable. For many months a small core, drawn initially from the IRB and subsequently supported by some within both the Volunteer movement and James Connolly's Irish Citizen Army, had planned a general insurrection, based in Dublin but spreading throughout the country. Motivated by various ideals but imbued with the common belief that only an armed revolt could bring about the independence of Ireland from the rest of the United Kingdom, they had sought support from Germany. The loss of 20,000 German rifles put an end to any realistic expectation of a successful military outcome to their plans for a general uprising and MacNeill's cancellation order greatly reduced the numbers available to occupy the GPO and other city-centre buildings in Dublin. Nonetheless, they decided to go ahead with a Rising in Dublin, agreeing to defer action by twenty-four hours to give time for the Dublin men to be mustered for Easter Monday.

When, one wonders, was it decided that the GPO would serve as headquarters of the rebellion and what was the reasoning behind the decision? The secrecy ensured that, on this occasion at least, agents and informers were not able to penetrate the core of the movement, and the execution of its leaders makes it impossible to answer these questions. The building certainly had defensive strengths, Johnston's central block possessing what Maurice Craig called an 'opulent severity', something that sounds like it would at least discourage potential besiegers. Its thick walls, basement vaults and extensive size suggest a structure that could well serve as a temporary fortress. Its roof-line commanded a strategic sweep of the city centre and would have made an assault difficult and costly. It occupied a large site, with good communication lines to the north and west and a less satisfactory route to the south, down Williams' Lane. Strategically, it offered a strong base from which sorties might be made to capture and support other buildings within its radius and, until the army cordon was drawn tightly around it, the GPO did serve this purpose. The symbolism of the Post Office may also have been a factor, for it could be said that the GPO was the civil representative of imperial power on the north side of the Liffey, a manifestation of government and the building that most prominently flew the flag, both literally and metaphorically, as the disburser of separation allowances, publicist for army recruitment and agent for investment.

What can be said with certainty is that someone within the inner circle that planned the Rising appreciated the importance of communications and the vital role played by the GPO in the control and provision not only of traditional mail channels but, more importantly, telegraph and telephone lines. Martin King, for instance, a cable joiner in the Post Office and an Irish Citizen Army man, recalled being asked by James Connolly towards the end of 1915 'if he wanted to cut communication with England, how would he go about it.'[3] That there was also an

---

3.   BMH WS 0543.

Robert Ballagh's recent interpretation of Walter Paget's Birth of the Republic *brings colour to the classic portrayal of coolness, control and conflict within the GPO.* (Courtesy of Robert Ballagh)

understanding of the broader public-relations issues is clear from the composition and printing of the Proclamation and *Irish War News*. This appreciation of the importance of communications is a notable feature in the thinking of the 1916 leaders, and their understanding of the place of the GPO at the heart of government communications was influential in their selection of the building as their headquarters. Men like J. J. Walsh, the future postmaster general of the Irish Free State, had been trained in wireless telegraphy by the Post Office and would have followed with some professional interest the famous instances when wireless messages, a few years before the Rising, had brought before the public the practical effects of technological advances. For example, the notorious murderer Dr Crippen, who had fled England on board the *Montrose* in 1910, was arrested before he landed in Canada, on foot of wireless communications from the

The GPO public office after the rebellion. (© Royal Mail Group Ltd 2014, Courtesy of the British Postal Museum & Archive)

ship to detectives at Scotland Yard. Even more famous is the case of the *Titanic*. The Morse SOS messages tapped out by her radio officer were picked up by the *Carpathia*, which despite being further away than many other ships, hurried to the rescue and was responsible for saving many of the 700 people who would otherwise have perished.

The practical knowledge and experience of the GPO's technical men among the rebels ensured that wireless transmission was immediately used as a communications and propaganda tool once the GPO had been secured. The Proclamation of a new Irish Republic was news that they wanted to broadcast as soon and as widely as possible and, to this end, the building at the corner of Lower Abbey Street and O'Connell Street – the site now occupied by the Grand Central Bar – was taken over. It had a strategic defensive role, of course, but its immediate interest for men like Walsh was the fact that it housed, just above Reis' jewellery shop, an organisation called The Irish School of Wireless, which not only offered tuition in wireless telegraphy but also dealt in wireless apparatus. Within it was a decommissioned transmitter that was swiftly made operational again and, with an aerial constructed on the roof of the building, the news of the

Rising was broadcast in Morse code to any ships that might happen to pick up the message and pass it on. Their intention, of course, was to make known to the world and, if possible, a sympathetic audience in America, what was happening in Dublin. News of the rebellion did indeed make its way quickly to the United States but there is no evidence that the daring and far-sighted experiment on the Lower Abbey Street corner was the means of transmission.[4]

The men who had been ordered to set up the wireless operation included Liam Daly, a London-born member of the largely English and Scottish Volunteer garrison based at Kimmage. He fixed up the aerial on the roof and many years later recalled hearing 'stones or pebbles striking the wall' close to him. Only when a chunk of the wall flew off beside him did he realise he was under fire from a sniper and he jumped down into the safety of the roof valley quicker than he ever

A view from the ruined public office through the roofless building towards the open sky. (© Royal Mail Group Ltd 2014, courtesy of the British Postal Museum & Archive)

did anything else. The men in the wireless school broadcast until Wednesday morning when army artillery fire made their situation untenable. They nonetheless did their best to save the transmitter, which they managed, using an up-turned table, to carry across Sackville Street and into the relative safety of the GPO. Thus it was that radio first gained its foothold in the GPO, although it would be more than a decade before broadcasting could be resumed.

That generation of revolutionaries sought control of radio and television stations; today's

---

4. News of the rebellion was, in fact, sent by Rosalie Rice in Kenmare post office to her Ring cousins, who worked at the Western Union cable station on Valentia Island, who forwarded it on to the United States. The coded cable, 'Mother operated on successfully today', was sent soon after the Rising began on Easter Monday and American papers were able to announce the dramatic news on the Tuesday before any official announcement was made in the House of Commons in London.

OPPOSITE: *The wonderfully finished telephone silence cabinet, which was placed in the GPO public office in 1916, would serve as a short-term cell for one prisoner during the Rising.*

have at their disposal the extraordinary power of the Internet and social media channels. Those who planned the Rising obviously understood the relevance and importance of the well-established telegraph network and the newer telephone system, and they were supported by a small group of GPO staff whose work meant they had an intimate knowledge of the city's communications network. The chief office of the GPO's engineering branch was located at the corner of Sackville Street and Middle Abbey Street, just a few yards down the road from the GPO where Clarks shoe shop is now. Men like Richard Mulcahy, though based himself in Aldborough House, would have had opportunities to drop in to that office to check details of cable routing and pass on information of potential use to the rebels. Indeed Mulcahy, before he joined Thomas Ashe in the attack on the RIC barracks at Ashbourne, had cut the telegraph and telephone wires that ran parallel to the Great Northern Railway line to Belfast.

Another Post Office man, Seán Byrne, recalled that on the Wednesday of Holy Week, Diarmuid Lynch, who had begun as a boy clerk in Cork post office, chaired a meeting attended by some of the GPO's engineering staff at which he announced that 'a special squad was being

The ruins of the sorting office in the GPO. (© Royal Mail Group Ltd 2014, courtesy of the British Postal Museum & Archive)

2.30 pm. Supg. Engineer, North Wales District confirms
= the Wersin telegram by telephone.

12.38

POST OFFICE TELEGRAPHS.

Service Message.

OFFICE STAMP.

Prefix _____ Rec'd _____.M. | Sent at _____.M. | Office

Code _____ From _____ | To _____ | Date 4.4.16 191

Words _____ By _____ | By _____

TO

Accy S P O H

P.O. Dublin taken possession
of today at noon by
Sinn Feiners — Sorting office
instrument room
railway stations also

Signature of
Sender.
(Not to be signalled.)

FROM

(5094). Wt. 10837-786. 1,500,000. 6/14. Wy. & S., Ltd. Sch. 68.

TO

Somersall of Engineers
amcif St

Signature of
Sender.
(Not to be signalled.)

FROM

(5094). Wt. 10837-786. 1,500,000. 6/14. Wy. & S., Ltd. Sch. 68.

War Office & Admiralty informed.

formed', which would cut communications 'so as to isolate the city'.[5] On Good Friday morning, two other staff members, Andy Fitzpatrick and Martin King, took a stroll around the city centre noting manholes and junctions of particular importance – places like the Lombard Street corner, which carried a special direct wire between Dublin Castle and London, and the Palace Street junction, which contained a host of police wires.

The severing of many important lines on Easter Monday morning was very successful, giving the rebels time to establish their positions and disrupting a government response that might otherwise have stifled the Rising before it had got under way.[6] The insurgents had also planned to capture the GPO's main telephone exchange in Crown Alley, off Dame Street in Dublin, but on Easter Monday 1916, confusion from the previous day's countermanding orders, scarcity of men and perhaps a little bad luck destroyed what had been a bold plan. There appears to have been no consideration given by the rebels to using the GPO's pneumatic tube system, a tube network much like those that once operated in some large department stores and that connected the GPO with its telegraph branch offices in College Green, the Custom House and the Four Courts. It might well have been used to supplement, at a reduced level of personal risk, the bravery of the various young men and women who acted as dispatch couriers between the GPO and other rebel positions. Attempts by the rebels to use the GPO's telegraph and telephone network for the purpose of encouraging insurrection elsewhere were quickly frustrated by the ingenuity and courage of loyal Post Office staff who were alive to the danger and closed or rerouted vulnerable circuits. The exploitation and control of communication channels, both traditional and technological, is a minor but fascinating research path that emerges from a study of Easter Week and it demonstrates a keen appreciation in the minds of the 1916 leaders of the critical importance of the GPO as Ireland's communications hub. This is why the Post Office mattered and why, more than any other reason, the GPO became the headquarters of the 1916 leaders.

When the rebels rushed into the GPO's public office shortly after midday on Easter Monday, there were a few customers going about their business. Their reaction may, at first, have been one

---

5. BMH WS 0579.

6. The pivotal role of GPO staff, both in disrupting and repairing communication channels, is a subject I examined in *Business as Usual: GPO Staff in 1916.*

of perplexed amusement and a resigned tolerance, perhaps, of the antics of those who enjoyed playing soldiers. However, as guns were brandished, windows smashed and barricades erected, those who could must have left the building as fast as possible. A couple of prisoners were taken, including a Lieutenant Chalmers, an off-duty soldier who happened to have gone into the GPO just before it was occupied. Perhaps he was the soldier whom James Stephens records went into the Post Office and asked the rebels for two penny stamps in the mistaken belief that their uniforms were postal uniforms.[7] He was searched for arms, tied up and bundled into the elaborate telephone kiosk in the main office. Post Office records, however, make clear that the building was not cleared nearly as quickly as some accounts have claimed, and the long-held belief that the GPO was taken without a shot being fired is untrue.

This 1915 plan of the GPO's top floor shows the telegraph Instrument Room and the northern and southern corridors through which the 1916 rebels made their attack after GPO staff and the Instrument Room guard refused to surrender to them. (Courtesy of the Office of Public Works)

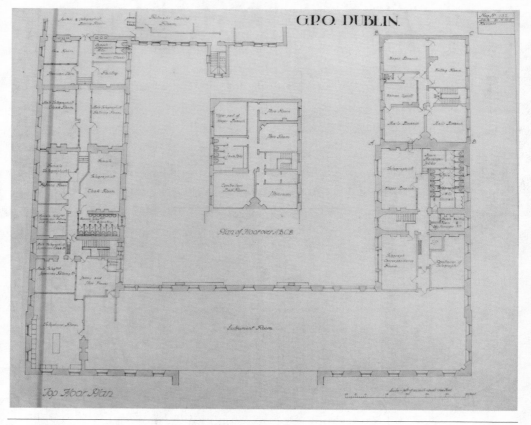

7.   Stephens, J., *The Insurrection in Dublin*, (Maunsel, Dublin, 1916), p. 28.

Upstairs in the GPO, staff in the telegraph office were the first to realise that something unusual was afoot when many of their lines suddenly went dead, having just been cut by GPO technical staff. Samuel Guthrie, whose Post Office career had begun in Ballybrophy over forty-five years before, was the superintendent on duty that day, and his description of the attack on the telegraph Instrument Room, from inside the GPO itself, is the first eyewitness account of the start of the rebellion. His report, and those of other GPO staff, are of great interest and reveal that the occupation of the GPO was not achieved quite as easily or as quickly as has been generally thought. It is worth turning to his account for a description of events:

> At 12 noon (I) a great many of the wires – including all the cross channel wires – became disconnected, apparently close up. At 12.10 pm I was informed that the Sinn Fein Volunteers were taking possession of the Public Counter and after a short time I heard the breaking of glass in the lower storey. On looking out of a window in the Telephone Room I saw that the windows of the Public Office and other windows looking into Sackville Street were being smashed, the fragments of glass falling on to and covering the pavement, and several members of the Sinn Fein party stood round the public entrance with rifles and revolvers. I at once got Mr P.I. Kelly to 'phone to Headquarters of the Army Command, the Police Office in the Castle, and also to Marlboro' Barracks asking for assistance.[8]

The floorplan illustrated here helps to clarify the location of the Instrument Room and the position of the Telephone Room from which Guthrie was able to look out and see the glass falling from the smashed windows. One of the women looking on from Sackville Street is quoted as saying, 'Glory be to God. The divils are smashing all the lovely windows,' and her indignation would have touched a chord with those looking down from Guthrie's window.[9]

Once the public office had been cleared, a Volunteer party headed upstairs to continue the task of emptying the building, and we can turn again to Guthrie for help in picturing the scene:

> At 12.30 pm I was informed by the Sergt. of the Guard that the Rebels were forcing the stairs leading from Henry Street to the Instrument Room and he asked me to obtain assistance for him. I explained to him what we had already done to obtain assistance. The guard consisted of a Sergeant and 4 men. The passage leading from the head of the stairs to the Instrument Room was then barricaded from the inside by filling it with chairs, wastepaper boxes etc. in order to delay the

---

8. British Postal Museum & Archive (BPMA) Post 31/80B. The time reference (I) here is to Dublin or Irish time which was twenty-five minutes behind Greenwich (G) time. The GPO, for telegraph purposes, kept Greenwich time but Dublin Mean Time otherwise and the difference can give rise to confusion. Dublin time, which had been established under the Definition of Time Act in 1880, was abolished in October 1916.

9. Brennan-Whitmore, W. J., *Dublin Burning: The Easter Rising from Behind the Barricades* (Gill & Macmillan, Dublin, 1996), p. 39.

The ruins of the GPO kitchen where Cumann na mBan women and some prisoners worked together preparing food for the rebel garrison. (© Royal Mail Group Ltd 2014, courtesy of the British Postal Museum & Archive)

entry of the attackers as much as possible, the guard of 1 Sergeant and 4 men standing inside the Instrument Room prepared to receive the rebels if they broke through the obstructions.[10]

The military guard on the Telegraph Room seems to have done all that it could to prevent the entry of the attacking Volunteers. Another member of staff, William Pemberton, adds the detail that the guard, though lacking ammunition for their guns, fixed bayonets and stood on either side of the northern entrance door to withstand the attack. The attacking party did not, it would seem, enter into any discussion at this stage but attempted instead to force an entrance through the corridor leading to the Instrument Room. 'Several volleys,' records Guthrie, 'were fired by the Rebels through the passage into the Instrument Room,' and Pemberton is able to add that

---

10. BPMA Post 31/80B.

he 'saw the Sergt. stagger as if wounded'. The resistance offered at this end of the Instrument Room may have prompted the Volunteers to send another group to attack by the southern door. This strategy proved more successful and, writes Guthrie:

> A short time before 1 pm a party of the Rebels gained an entrance to the Instrument Room by the Southern Corridor after having passed through the Dining Room. As there was only one sentry on that corridor he was easily overpowered.

Guthrie must have been a worried man but as the attack began on the northern corridor, he did his best to shield the female staff there from the shooting, instructing them to 'go into their Retiring Room' and, with rather touching avuncular concern in the circumstances, to 'put on their outdoor apparel in case they would have to leave the building'. The female staff, however, were not without their own local heroine in the form of Katherine Gordon, assistant supervisor of telegraphs, whom Pemberton notes:

> declined to leave the Instrument Room when the rebels occupied it until she had attended to the wounds of the Sergeant of the Military Guard, who had been injured in his plucky effort to defend the Southern entrance to the room.[11]

The sergeant's wounds were more than superficial and the two, having given their word to return to the GPO, were permitted to go down to Jervis Street Hospital to receive professional attention. True to their promise, they did return and, while the sergeant was kept a prisoner, Miss Gordon, having shown both bravery and compassion for the wounded soldier, was allowed to leave the building at about five o'clock. This remarkable incident, which reflects great credit on the integrity of rebels and staff alike, is one of what must be several personal stories that do not feature in the standard accounts of the Rising. Another is the rather touching and very human story of the young GPO clerk who, on being ordered out and having left her bicycle in the basement, was more concerned about the trouble she might get into for abandoning official property than any imminent danger to herself.

Guthrie's old-fashioned gallantry in relation to his female staff is in keeping with his attitude to those who had attacked the Post Office. Informed that an officer of the besieging force wanted to see him about the withdrawal of his staff, he 'sent word to him that I would not hold any parley with him as I did not recognise he had any right to be where he was'. The officer, subsequently identified as The O'Rahilly and accompanied by a few supporters, entered the Instrument Room a few minutes later. Guthrie reports that each carried a revolver and that the officer 'told all the officials in the room

---

11. *Ibid.*

POBLACHT NA H EIREANN.

THE PROVISIONAL GOVERNMENT
OF THE
IRISH REPUBLIC
TO THE PEOPLE OF IRELAND.

IRISHMEN AND IRISHWOMEN : In the name of God and of the dead generations from which she receives her old tradition of nationhood, Ireland, through us, summons her children to her flag and strikes for her freedom.

Having organised and trained her manhood through her secret revolutionary organisation, the Irish Republican Brotherhood, and through her open military organisations, the Irish Volunteers and the Irish Citizen Army, having patiently perfected her discipline, having resolutely waited for the right moment to reveal itself, she now seizes that moment, and, supported by her exiled children in America and by gallant allies in Europe, but relying in the first on her own strength, she strikes in full confidence of victory.

We declare the right of the people of Ireland to the ownership of Ireland, and to the unfettered control of Irish destinies, to be sovereign and indefeasible. The long usurpation of that right by a foreign people and government has not extinguished the right, nor can it ever be extinguished except by the destruction of the Irish people. In every generation the Irish people have asserted their right to national freedom and sovereignty ; six times during the past three hundred years they have asserted it in arms. Standing on that fundamental right and again asserting it in arms in the face of the world, we hereby proclaim the Irish Republic as a Sovereign Independent State, and we pledge our lives and the lives of our comrades-in-arms to the cause of its freedom, of its welfare, and of its exaltation among the nations.

The Irish Republic is entitled to, and hereby claims, the allegiance of every Irishman and Irishwoman. The Republic guarantees religious and civil liberty, equal rights and equal opportunities to all its citizens, and declares its resolve to pursue the happiness and prosperity of the whole nation and of all its parts, cherishing all the children of the nation equally, and oblivious of the differences carefully fostered by an alien government, which have divided a minority from the majority in the past.

Until our arms have brought the opportune moment for the establishment of a permanent National Government, representative of the whole people of Ireland and elected by the suffrages of all her men and women, the Provisional Government, hereby constituted, will administer the civil and military affairs of the Republic in trust for the people.

We place the cause of the Irish Republic under the protection of the Most High God, Whose blessing we invoke upon our arms, and we pray that no one who serves that cause will dishonour it by cowardice, inhumanity, or rapine. In this supreme hour the Irish nation must, by its valour and discipline and by the readiness of its children to sacrifice themselves for the common good, prove itself worthy of the august destiny to which it is called.

Signed on Behalf of the Provisional Government,

THOMAS J. CLARKE,

SEAN MacDIARMADA,   THOMAS MacDONAGH,
P. H. PEARSE,   EAMONN CEANNT,
JAMES CONNOLLY.   JOSEPH PLUNKETT.

An Post's copy of the 1916 Proclamation is on display in its Letters, Lives & Liberty *exhibition in the GPO.*

to clear out at once at the same time questioning each one as to whether he carried arms'.[12] Pemberton's account once again adds a touch of colour to the older man's more formal narrative:

> A rebel ordered us out of the building with the remark 'sorry to disturb you gentlemen' and made some additional remark like 'this is the first and last act'.[13]

The female staff had already left the room, and by 1.31 p.m. (G) the men were on their way downstairs to be 'let out of the main gate at Prince's Street by the rebel guard'. Pemberton immediately made his way to Brunswick Street (now Pearse Street) police station to report the matter, but the police there, displaying a rather remarkable lack of interest, redirected him to Store Street, telling him to make his report there.

The 1916 leaders were conscious that they needed to have a statement prepared that might justify the militant, undemocratic step they were taking, and one of Pearse's first actions, soon after entering the GPO, was to come to the front of the building and read a document proclaiming the Irish Republic a sovereign, independent state. His few listeners heard him with a largely bemused indifference, unaware that they were witnessing the beginning of events that would profoundly influence Irish history. The Proclamation is a rare document and very few are known to have survived. Each has individual associations, with An Post's copy, for instance, bearing in the top left hand corner the inscription 'Found in Dublin Easter 1916 by John Phillips'. One man in the GPO, later destined to become president of Ireland, was Seán T. O'Kelly. He was given the job of pasting up the Proclamations around the city centre, and realising, perhaps, that not many of them might survive the turmoil, he posted one to his aunt, in the pillar box a few yards from the GPO itself. With a short and understandable delay it was duly delivered and survives to this day. It is probable that a good proportion of the original print run of some 2,500 copies perished in the fires that destroyed the GPO, for there cannot have been time to post up more than a small number around the city. According to the memory of Liam Robinson, who took part in the Rising, some of the remainder were put to immediate practical use.

> Early in Easter Week I was lying wounded in the Guard Room of the GPO which had previously been occupied by the British guard, together with a British soldier who was badly wounded. I had nothing under my head, until a Cumann na mBan girl came in with a bundle of Republican Proclamations, probably a couple of hundred, out of which she made me a nice pillow.[14]

---

12. BPMA Post 31/80B. Guthrie, writing to his superior, J. J. Kenny, in his report of 6 May 1916, identifies the officer as 'a Mr Connolly' but this has been crossed out and replaced with 'The O'Rahilly'.

13. *Ibid.*

14. *Sunday Press* (23 December 1951). I am indebted to Liam Robinson's great nephew for bringing this reference to my attention. The British soldier mentioned may well be the member of the Instrument Room guard who was wounded, brought to Jervis Street by the GPO's Miss Gordon and then brought back to become a prisoner.

LOWER ABBEY STREET, SHOW

Next to Post Office, the

ROYAL HIBERNIAN ACADEMY·

historic loss of the fires.

PREVIOUS PAGES: *The Lower Abbey Street ruins of the Royal Hibernian Academy, set up through the generosity of Francis Johnston.*

The manuscript of the Proclamation was brought by Thomas MacDonagh to James Connolly in the old Liberty Hall in Abbey Street on Easter Sunday morning and shown to the printer and two compositors who worked for Connolly. Christopher Brady, the printer, in the statement he made to the Bureau of Military History remembered the occasion and recalled that 'As a humble workman' he 'considered it a great honour to be entrusted to do such a heroic job'. Later that day the three men began work, and by 9 p.m. they had a first proof ready for Connolly, which he checked against the manuscript. Theirs was a dangerous task and their conditions were difficult: they had to struggle with an old and dilapidated printing press, inferior paper and insufficient type. Shortage of type meant that the Proclamation had to be printed in two halves. This is immediately apparent from the marked contrast between the lightly inked top half of the document and the more heavily inked bottom half. The men printed the top half, redistributed their type and set it again for the bottom half. The half-printed sheets were reinserted into the press and the lower portion added to that already printed. Certain letters, notably *e*, were in short supply, and different fonts had to be used (see, for instance, the words 'thr*e*e hundr*e*d y*e*ars' in the third paragraph). What looks like a capital E in the fifth-line 'TO THE' is actually an *F* with an additional leg made from sealing wax joined on to it. As a sample of their art, the printers might have been less than happy with the Proclamation but, in terms of patience and ingenuity under difficult and dangerous conditions, it must rank as a very accomplished piece of work. It was the early hours of Easter Monday morning before they had their work done and copies ready for distribution around the city later in the day.[15]

Solemn and high-minded in tone, the Proclamation is thought to be largely the work of Patrick Pearse, but there is a radical edge to the content – guarantees of religious and civil liberty, equal rights and opportunities for all citizens and votes for women as well as men – which points to the influence of James Connolly, the labour leader and founder of the Irish Citizen Army. The document, therefore, is more than a justification and a call to arms – it is a statement of belief and a vision of a better future for all Irish men and women. While the initial invocation beginning with 'Irishmen and Irishwomen', the striking words about 'cherishing all the children of the nation equally' and a few other phrases are well known, it is not, for all the respect shown to it, a document that is often read through. This is a pity, as there is original thinking in the Proclamation and an idealism that transcends the period and the event for which

---

15   On the printing of the Proclamation, see J. J. Bouch's article in *Publications of the Bibliographical Society of Ireland* (1936) vol. 5, no. 3.

it was composed. It may be that those who wrote it had an eye on posterity and hoped it might serve as an enduring vision to encourage and inspire Irish people at home and abroad. In the midst of a world war, however, in which many thousands of Irishmen were fighting, those who put their names to a Proclamation drawing attention to the support received from Germany – the unnamed 'gallant allies in Europe' – must have known the inevitable consequence of their actions, if the rebellion failed.

For the rank and file members of the GPO garrison the week started quietly enough. The government's response was hampered by the fact that many of its senior officials were on leave, and the unfortunate Lancers, who sauntered into Sackville Street, can have had no intention of retaking the GPO. They were met by a volley from the GPO, which killed some soldiers and sent the rest back to their barracks in a hurry. The rebels concentrated on strengthening their position, obtaining supplies and discouraging those citizens of Dublin who saw in the situation an opportunity for unrestricted access to the merchandise of the city's more prestigious shops. The high-minded aims of the rebels sat uncomfortably with the reality of daily life for those who lived in the streets surrounding the GPO, and the looters, it was felt, were rather letting down the new Republic.

The Easter Monday eyewitness accounts of the GPO staff are the earliest available of what it was like in the GPO, but they of course cover only the very start of the rebellion. There are other interesting narratives that, while not as immediate, provide an insight into what went on inside the building. Moira Regan, for instance, was a member of Cumann na mBan and she was interviewed for *The New York Times*, which on 20 August 1916 carried her account of the rebellion. It is not an impartial account, nor wholly accurate, but it does paint a picture of the GPO interior. She arrived at the GPO on the evening of Easter Monday and recalls finding that 'the windows were barricaded with bags of sand, and at each of them were two men with rifles'. The next day she joined other women in the kitchen, fifteen or so, making 'big sandwiches of beef and cheese' and handing out 'milk and beef tea'. She found the kitchen well supplied with 'enough provisions to last for three weeks'. Working with her in the kitchen were ten English soldiers, 'that is, they wore the English uniform, but they were Irishmen', men who had been captured and who 'peeled potatoes and washed dishes uncomplainingly'. Captured officers, who were under the care of The O'Rahilly, were held in another room, and on the Wednesday, she was instructed by O'Rahilly to act as postman and deliver a letter to the wife of one of the officers at her home in Drumcondra. 'It was,' Regan recounts, 'a good long walk, and I can tell you that I blessed that English officer and his wife before I delivered that letter!' Joyce Kilmer, the journalist who interviewed Moira Regan for the paper, portrays her as a 'slight, gray-eyed girl' with the 'charming flavour of County Wexford in her manner and in her voice' and contrasts this vulnerable frailty with her GPO experience, when she had 'breathed air redolent with gunpowder and heard the groans of men torn by shot and shell.'

It is this type of dramatic narrative that helped to create the enduring and popular image of the GPO as a beleaguered fortress under siege, its defenders hopelessly outnumbered but undaunted. The narrative, however, did not go unchallenged at the time and a few days after the appearance of the 'Irish Girl Rebel Tells of Dublin Fighting' piece, a correspondent, Susan Kinch, wrote to the editor, who published her letter on 28 August. Acknowledging that the scholars and dreamers of the rebellion loved Ireland, she put the case of those other Irishmen who were fighting in the Great War and 'who love her [Ireland] not less passionately and wholeheartedly' but who could only see in the 'whole episode a disgraceful plot to sell our country to a foreign foe'.

Among Irish people as a whole, reaction to the Rising was overwhelmingly negative and even within the nationalist camp there were several for whom a rebellion that had no chance of success was a pointless waste of life and was morally repugnant. Inside the GPO itself, this view was communicated to Pearse by Louise Gavan Duffy, secretary of Cumann na mBan, on Easter Monday when she made her way to the GPO:

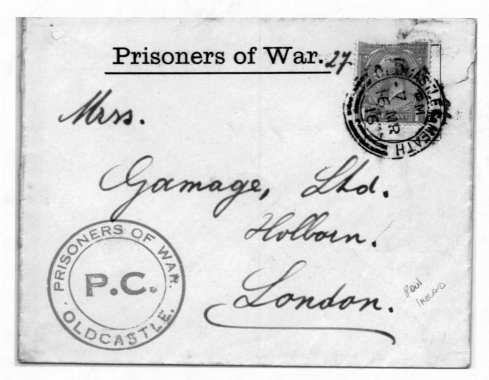

A letter with prisoner-of-war markings sent from Oldcastle a month before the Rising to the jewellery firm of Gammage in London. Oldcastle in County Meath was the site of a prisoner-of-war camp for enemy aliens during the First World War.

I was brought into the Post Office and I saw Mr Pearse. He was as calm and courteous as ever … I said to him that I wanted to be in the field but I felt that the Rebellion was a frightful mistake, that it could not possibly succeed and it was, therefore, wrong.[16]

She spent the week working in the kitchen in the GPO and on Friday was in the party that made its way with the wounded from the GPO yard at the back of the building via houses and the Coliseum Theatre to Jervis Street Hospital. Hers is one of the many witness statements which, though compiled many years after the Rising following the creation of the Bureau of Military History in 1947, help to create a picture of what actually went on in the GPO during the Rising. Other insights can be gained from the recently published records compiled for the purpose of establishing the pension entitlements of those who participated in the Rising. Margaret (Peggy) Downie was one of the women who worked with Louise Gavan Duffy in the GPO kitchen

Some GPO staff who were on duty during the Rising were awarded extra leave in recognition of the dangers they had undergone and the special efforts made to restore normal service. References to 'Rebellion leave' occur occasionally in record books of the period.

16. BMH WS 216 file no. S/196.

during the week. Not content to go home after she had spent a night in Jervis Street Hospital, she reported for further duty in Jacob's biscuit factory. Her correspondence with the Department of Defence is interesting in that, having been awarded a pension, she wrote to the Department from Twickenham in England on 9 October 1962 generously relinquishing her entitlement with the words, 'I do not now need the money and so feel I should not continue taking it.'[17]

Fintan Murphy, a member of the 4th Battalion of the Irish Volunteers, made a statement to the Bureau in 1950, but he was able to rely on an account he had prepared and broadcast from Radio Éireann's studio in the GPO in 1936. It claims attention from the start:

> Twenty years ago tonight and almost within a week of this date, I stood, with a rifle in my hand on the roof of the G.P.O.

Murphy and his company, under the command of Éamonn Bulfin, had arrived late from Rathfarnham into the GPO and, as they knocked at the door in Prince's Street, they were warned to prepare to receive the Lancer party that was in Sackville Street. Firing from inside the building, however, ensured the retreat of these soldiers before they got very far down the street. The key to the entrance on Prince's Street had been mislaid and Murphy's group had to clamber in through a window, Éamonn Bulfin having broken not only the glass but his rifle as well in the process. Having got into the GPO they found themselves in a locked sorting room and Bulfin had to shoot the lock in order to get his men into the public office. Transferring their homemade shrapnel bombs into the building through a window was a delicate job, and an injury was caused when a bomb was dropped while being passed inside. These sobering incidents must have forcefully brought home to them the danger and grave seriousness of the enterprise in which they were engaged.

Bulfin and his company were subsequently assigned to the roof, where they observed developments from behind the safety of the GPO parapet. Liam Daly, on the instructions of James Connolly, who had met Daly once and remembered that he had technical expertise, had set up on the first day of the Rising a direct telephone link between the roof and the command post in the public office by running a wire through the ceilings, enabling news of any attack to be relayed instantly to the men in the public office. At the Prince's Street corner of the GPO Éamonn Bulfin hoisted what he called the 'ordinary Irish flag, green with the harp, and in white letters (inscribed) across the middle were the words "Irish Republic"'.[18] Meals were taken in the canteen beside him on the top floor and with the weather 'fine and dry that week' he found 'sleeping on the roof was no great hardship'. He was still there on Wednesday morning when

---

17. Military Service Pensions (MSP) 34REF542.
18. BMH WS 497.

The basement fireproof chamber under the GPO portico lived up to its name and the cabling was found unharmed after the insurrection. (© Royal Mail Group Ltd 2014, courtesy of the British Postal Museum & Archive)

some ineffectual shelling began from the river and D'Olier Street. He recalled Fr Flanagan, a Marlborough Street priest, bravely clambering over the roof to deliver a general absolution in view of what seemed to be the start of a serious attack. In the event, no attack came, and Murphy was sent down to reinforce the public office where he caught a glimpse of the general staff, including James Connolly 'reclining on a stretcher bed on account of the wound in his leg which was certainly worrying him a lot by now in spite of attention'.

The main public office of the GPO was the command centre where reports were made and orders issued and it was Connolly who was most active in directing operations, encouraging his men and taking a personal interest in their welfare. Walter Carpenter, for instance, was a member of the Boys' Corps of the Citizen Army and, as he was ill, Connolly sent him home on Wednesday night of Easter Week along with other boys who were under eighteen years of age. Carpenter had been one of those whose duty it had been to guard the printing press in Liberty Hall in the weeks before the rebellion. The examination of his pension application case in 1936 brings to light tensions that persisted between the Volunteer elements of the nationalist movement and the Irish Citizen Army people. The corroborating evidence and statements sought in support of Carpenter, for instance, include speculation on whether he had actually been in the Four Courts during the Civil War since 'he was an alleged Communist' and 'would not join the Volunteers because we were not holding a class war'.[19] In her statement to the advisory committee in December 1936, Mary Adrien, a Cumann na mBan member who had acted as an emissary between Thomas Ashe and the GPO early in Easter Week, shows that she was less concerned with this sort of political distinction. In the aftermath of the action at Ashbourne, she states that she provided first aid 'to both sides – both friend and enemy'.[20] Connolly would no doubt have approved of her sensible attitude, for after he had been wounded by a ricochet bullet he was treated in the GPO by a captured British Army doctor, Captain Mahony, who regarded himself first and foremost as a doctor and who recalled, much later, Connolly's remark to him, 'You know, you're the best thing we've captured this week.'[21]

Just off the main hall in the primary sorting room, a field hospital, staffed by Cumann na mBan women, had been set up. While many of the women who took part in the rebellion did work in the hospital or the kitchen, some played a crucial and dangerous role as dispatch messengers between rebel positions. A scrapbook in the National Library includes one cutting entitled *Daring Girl Rebels* in which an unnamed Red Cross nurse asserts that 'Many of the women were snipers' – certainly an exaggeration – but her memory of seeing one girl set off from the GPO is borne out by fact:

> I saw Count Plunkett's son ... come to the front door of the Post Office and wish her good luck as he shook hands with her before she made the reckless dash to take Connolly's dispatch back to her own headquarters.[22]

Pearse, in comparison with Connolly, seems to have been much more detached from events, Min Ryan recalling that he:

> spent most of his time in the front part of the Post Office. It was nearly the same then as it is now ... there was a counter where you could get stamps. All these young fellows, the Plunketts, Mick Collins, and crowds of others ... were manning the windows. The Headquarters staff sat there talking quietly.[23]

---

19. MSP 34REF8789.
20. MSP 34REF152.
21. Caulfield, M., *The Easter Rebellion* (Gill & Macmillan, Dublin, 1995), p. 234.
22. NLI Ms 32,695.
23. BMH WS 399.

This view of the ruined shell of the GPO is from the vantage point of Nelson's Pillar. (© Royal Mail Group Ltd 2014, courtesy of the British Postal Museum & Archive)

As he sat there in the GPO, amidst the postal fittings, stamps and account books of daily Dublin life, did Pearse ever doubt the wisdom of the course he had taken? His influence as an intellectual, poet and gifted teacher, particularly on the minds of the boys and young men in his school, was considerable and he must at times have questioned, within himself at least, what he was doing. On the other hand, the tales of heroism and self-sacrifice that Pearse found in the literature of the Gaelic Revival were the same stories that made army recruitment so easy, at least in the early stages of the Great War:

> Then out spake brave Horatius, the Captain of the Gate:
> 'To every man upon this earth, death cometh soon or late;
> And how can man die better than facing fearful odds,
> For the ashes of his fathers and the temples of his Gods.'

Macaulay's Horatius, defending Rome against Lars Porsena, is also the embodiment of Cuchulain, single-handedly defending Ulster against the armies of Connacht. To the valour and sacrifice of heroes of old, Pearse added a deeply felt Christian belief in the potency of sacrifice and resurrection at Eastertide. The rebellion, in his mind a rising in the Christian sense, has been placed under the protection of the 'Most High God' whose blessing the Proclamation invokes on the enterprise. No wonder, perhaps, that, as Min Ryan noticed, he 'sat out there in the front on one of the high stools, and people would come and talk to him'.

Communication with those commanding other strongpoints in the neighbourhood was relatively easy at first but as the week progressed the army, augmented by reinforcements from England, poured into the city as a tight cordon gradually closed in on the insurgents. Until it was destroyed, a rather ingenious wire pulley system operated from the GPO across Sackville Street to the Imperial Hotel directly opposite, and messages in cans were sent back and forth without endangering lives – a nice little postal innovation by the men in the GPO.

From their vantage points on the roof of the Post Office, from which flew the flags of the Irish Republic they had proclaimed, the rebels made sure that any frontal assault on the building would be strongly repulsed. On Thursday the expectation within the GPO was that an assault was imminent and it was decided to strengthen the front of the building with coal from the basement cellars. Nothing was readily to hand, however, in which to transport the coal until Fintan Murphy and his companions broke open the mailbag store room. 'We burst it open …

Such was the intensity of the heat in the fires that destroyed the GPO that copper wires melted in their casings. (© Royal Mail Group Ltd 2014, courtesy of the British Postal Museum & Archive)

and found neatly piled up hundreds of new, clean mail bags.'[24] These were filled and used to strengthen the window barricades. The coal defences made a good, solid bullet-resistant wall, but as the fires burned closer, the notion of using coal as a bulwark must have struck some as less than inspired. In the event, a frontal assault on the GPO fortunately never came, but the artillery shells brought steady and increasing destruction.

Within the GPO itself additional lines of communication had been opened up on the Henry Street side of the building by boring through the GPO's exterior wall to the houses beyond. Frank Henderson, an officer in the 2nd Battalion of the Volunteers, provided in 1949 a lengthy and detailed statement to the Bureau of Military History on his background and involvement in the Rising. Much of this had been published before the general release of the witness statements in 2003 and shows that the preparations for the Rising, in terms of gathering the technical and theoretical knowledge necessary to mount an armed revolution, had been thorough. Henderson, for instance, mentions the fact that in line with the 'instructions which we had received during lectures, we staggered the breaches in the wall as far as possible'.[25] Henderson, having cleared out a caretaker from the premises, started work in Bewley's shop – located roughly where the JD Sports shop is today – while his brother Leo worked towards him from McDowell's jewellery shop, which was situated where the entrance to the GPO Arcade is now. Their task was made much easier by help from five brothers, four of whom were carpenters by trade. By Wednesday morning the work had been finished and the creation of this interior-communications line gave the rebels a strategic position in the Coliseum Theatre commanding the approach from Moore Street and a view on up to Parnell Street. Such work is a clear sign of careful military planning and evidence that the selection of the GPO and other buildings in the city had been no last-minute decision on the part of the IRB's strategists. In their planning for what was probably originally envisaged as a Dublin-led rebellion, there emerges a very sensible defensive pattern that successfully tied up a great many British Army troops. As a rebellion it was bound to fail but there is pragmatic soldiering here that must take its place alongside Pearse's more mystical sense of heroic sacrifice.

Fire as an enemy had probably been overlooked in the planning but large conflagrations had taken hold of both the Metropole Hotel and *The Freeman's Journal*'s premises in Prince's Street by Wednesday night. Some of the garrison slipped out the gate to free horses trapped in stables close to the newspaper's offices. 'The frightened animals,' Fintan Murphy remembered, 'stampeded up the street and gave the impression of a cavalry charge.' So realistic was the impression that the horses were fired on by the men on duty at the front of the GPO and a homemade bomb, about to be thrown by one of the men, was dropped on the floor but luckily failed to detonate.

---

24. BMH WS 370.
25. BMH WS 249.

The position grew steadily worse on Thursday, and by Friday morning the army's heavy guns had found the range of the GPO, and the roof and upper storeys along with much of Sackville Street were ablaze. Strenuous efforts were made to contain the fires and hoses were turned on them as they spread, but such was the intensity of the heat that water rapidly turned to steam and lead melted in the casings of the telegraph cabling. After a while the hoses became useless as the water supply ceased. It is a tribute both to the construction of the building and the bravery of those within it that they endured the conditions as long as they did, but it was clear that they could not long remain. Twelve of the fifteen women who had stayed in the Post Office, sixteen wounded and a few uninjured men, including Fr Flanagan and Captain Mahony, slowly made their way from the back of the GPO via roofs and tunnels into the Coliseum Theatre in Henry Street. Explosives that had been stored in the public office were transferred to the basement – a dangerous task for which John Twamley, a Post Office engineer, volunteered – and a fuse was positioned and laid so that the building might be blown up after evacuation of the garrison. Fortunately this did not happen.

As the evening drew in, Fintan Murphy recalled the whole garrison being assembled in the central courtyard of the GPO and being addressed by Pearse who spoke 'words of encouragement and praise for our defence of the position, told us that the staff had decided that the building was untenable and that we must seek positions elsewhere'.[26] The plan was to make their way out to a new strongpoint in Parnell Street but the cordon around the city centre was now so tight that this proved impossible. The O'Rahilly, with others, had tried to make some exploratory headway up Moore Street but had fallen, mortally wounded, in the attempt. In the first few days of the Rising he had managed to scribble a few encouraging lines to his wife: 'G.P.O. 6.15 p.m. All safe here so far. Things going well I believe in most places.' He had even received a reply from his son at home in Herbert Park. Despite the passage of a century, that letter, penned by a child and punctured by a small round hole, remains immensely moving:

26th April 1916

Dear Dada ... I heard from Nell and Anna that the volunteers are winning. I don't suppose they will ever get the G.P.O. for as long as you are in command.[27]

The prisoners, for whom O'Rahilly had had responsibility during the week and with whom he had shaken hands before he led his men out of the GPO, also left the Post Office and fled across Henry Street to take their chances in the lanes on the far side. 'We evacuated in small groups, and dashed across Henry Street into Henry Place, which was right across from the Henry Street

---

26. BMH WS 370.
27. NLI Ms 21,854.

The famous Moore Street surrender photograph showing Pearse standing before Brigadier General Lowe and his Irish adjutant, Captain de Courcy Wheeler. (Courtesy of Mercier Press Archive)

exit gate of the Post Office,' Murphy remembered. At last, Pearse and Connolly, the latter on a stretcher, left the GPO and crossed to Moore Lane with the intention of occupying another strongpoint in Parnell Street. Behind them, the GPO lay in ruins, its granite walls, in the eyes of one reporter, 'like the walls of a skeleton skull' and its core 'nothing but smouldering debris'. The flagpole, on which the flag with the words IRISH REPUBLIC had flown, finally began to bend under the heat of the fires and at 9.51 p.m. it slowly fell outwards towards the street. On Friday night and Saturday morning, tunnelling from house to house in Moore Street, desperate efforts were still being made to break out, but realising that further resistance would lead to more civilian deaths, Pearse decided to surrender. At 2.30 p.m. he gave up his sword to Brigadier General Lowe and his Irish aide-de-camp, Captain de Courcy Wheeler, at the corner of Moore Street. The rebellion was over.

Edward Delaney's stylised view of the ruined GPO was part of a set of commemorative stamps issued by the Post Office in 1966 to mark the fiftieth anniversary of the Rising.

Hanslip Fletcher's drawing of a largely unscathed GPO façade hides the damage suffered by the building in 1916.

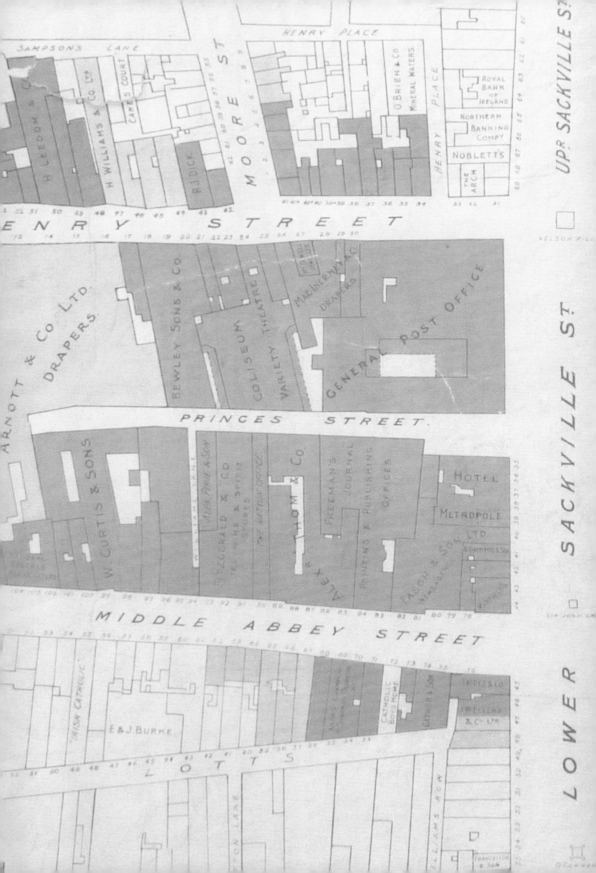

Rising from
the Ashes

❦ ❦

The restoration of the building is symbolic of the new Order. As this building has come back to us, renewed and beautiful, so is the Irish nation progressing in the path of prosperity and peace.

W. T. Cosgrave speaking at the reopening of the GPO in 1929

❦ ❦

The death and destruction of Easter Week, combined with the execution of the Rising's leaders, had a profound impact on the city and its citizens, but for the people in the GPO it was a case of picking up the pieces as soon as possible. Norway, the secretary, had been under pressure from the Lord Lieutenant, Lord Wimborne, and his former Post Office boss, Sir Mathew Nathan, now undersecretary in the Irish administration, to reintroduce some sort of postal service in Dublin during Easter Week itself, but he felt, quite rightly, that the situation was far too dangerous for this, observing that 'the appearance of a Mail Car or any person in official uniform on the streets would ... have been simply madness'. With access to the city virtually impossible and sniping 'almost universal', his view seems quite reasonable, but he notes that it was accepted by his political superiors 'somewhat reluctantly'.[1] Conscious that some sort of official enquiry into their stewardship would inevitably follow the suppression of the rebellion, they were

---

1. BPMA Post 31/80.

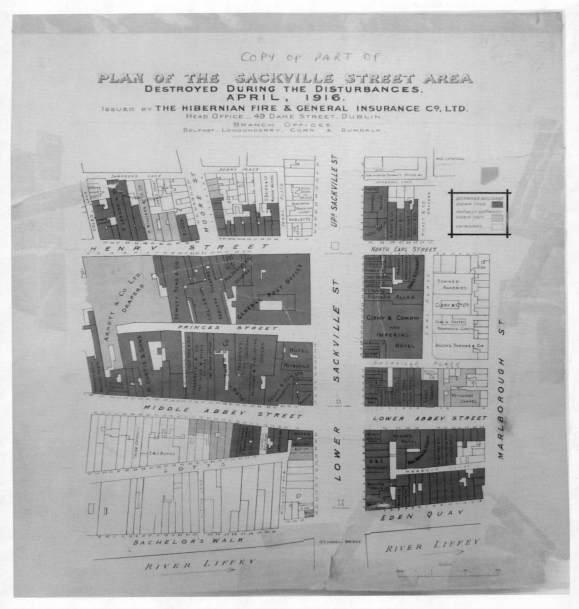

The extent of the destruction in the city centre is clearly shown in this map produced by the Hibernian Fire & General Insurance Company. (Courtesy of the Office of Public Works)

probably keen to play down the significance of events in Dublin by demonstrating a swift return to normality.

A small mail had actually been dispatched to England on the evening of 29 April, the very day Pearse surrendered, but Norway, writing to his boss in London on 30 April, made it quite clear that he was not prepared to take responsibility for ordering the resumption of services 'unless and until the military authorities give me clear assurances of the *reasonable* – not absolute – safety of my staff'. Enough dangers, he felt, had been risked already by 'those whose obligations were for the moment of essential importance to the public safety' but he was not prepared to call on his staff 'to risk their lives merely to get a little correspondence into England a day or two sooner'.[2]

Within a few days of the end of the Rising, the extent of the destruction became apparent and it was clear that the GPO, so recently gleaming from its renovation, would be useless from any operational aspect. With commendable speed, however, a temporary sorting office

A. H. Norway, secretary of the Irish Post Office in 1916.

was established within the Rotunda buildings at the top of Sackville Street. Part of the complex was at that time an ice rink and the area was rapidly modified so that sorting and delivery work had resumed by the morning of 3 May. Mrs Norway, whose own account of Easter Week in Dublin provides a vivid and perceptive commentary, was highly impressed with the industry of the staff – 'a regular hive of bees' – busy sorting with no proper fittings but what they 'had contrived for themselves out of seats, benches and old scenery'.[3] Just three days after the end of hostilities, the GPO's physical infrastructure had been reorganised and two daily deliveries reinstated in Dublin. Telegraph work, which had been maintained so conscientiously by Post Office staff throughout the Rising, was put on a proper footing, with the top floor of the GPO's

---

2. BPMA Post 56/177.

3. Norway, Mrs H., *The Sinn Féin Rebellion As I Saw It* (Smith, Elder & Co., London, 1916), p. 87. Her record of Easter Week was published in July 1916 in the form of a series of letters.

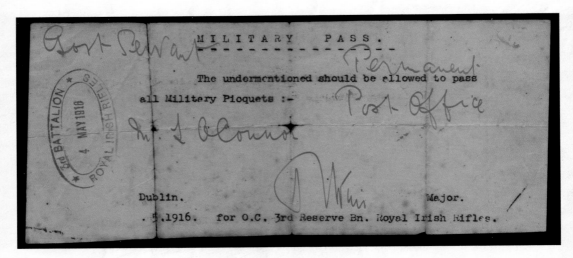

A pass issued by the military authorities to L. O'Connor of the GPO to allow him to go about his work.

A mailbag hung on a railing to act as an emergency post box after the Rising. (© Royal Mail Group Ltd 2014, courtesy of the British Postal Museum & Archive)

Parcels Office in Amiens Street being converted into a telegraph instrument room. Military restrictions remained on public access to the system, but the GPO's engineering staff had the new office ready for business by 9 May.

The GPO's accounting staff faced particular difficulties in relation to arrangements made to ensure the continued payment of old-age pensions and separation allowances to the wives of soldiers at the Front – an issue of particular importance to the army. As the relevant records had been destroyed, the accountant's office, having fallen victim to the fires started on the night the insurrection ended, had had to draw on details held elsewhere in order to prepare the payments. Norway requested an armoured car to accompany the staff who were to distribute the funds to the various branch and sub-offices in Dublin. His wife records the excitement when one of these homemade 'monsters' with a reinforced engine boiler mounted on a lorry chassis turned up outside the Royal Hibernian Hotel before proceeding to the Bank of Ireland to collect £10,000 in silver for delivery throughout the city.

Busy at work – GPO staff sorting in the temporary sorting office set up at the Rotunda. (© Royal Mail Group Ltd 2014, courtesy of the British Postal Museum & Archive)

OVERLEAF: *Workmen standing beside a consignment of blocks destined to be used in the rebuilding of the GPO.* (Courtesy of the National Library of Ireland)

The GPO continued to smoulder for several days, but as soon as possible the debris was carefully examined to see if anything could be salvaged from the wreckage. Very little was left. Post Office records and ledgers were reduced to 'a mound of what looked like solid white chalk', which Mrs Norway records 'felt like silk between my fingers'. Watching the workmen sift through the wreckage in her husband's office, she was reminded of the excavations at Pompeii and was delighted when among the ruins three little brooches were found: they had been given to her by her son when he was a boy. Elsewhere in the wreckage, money to the value of £185 was found and deposited in the savings bank. The accountant general in London, Sir Charles King, proposed to credit the appropriation-in-aid account if it remained unclaimed at the end of the year. He recommended a similar course in respect of the £149 10s. found on one of the prisoners arrested at the GPO. Official cash lost in the GPO during the Rising was estimated at £2,792 18s. 7d. Parcels and registered letters were destroyed, of course, and the question of compensation of customers arose. The solicitor's advice at the time was, however, unambiguously in favour of the Post Office:

> A common carrier who takes proper care is not liable to the owner of goods conveyed by him for loss occasioned by 'the act of God or the King's enemies'.[4]

While the loss of life, destruction of property and political consequences of the Rising occupied the minds of the public and GPO officials were occupied with the restoration of services, accountants in various branches of the civil service were considering how best to treat the destruction of the GPO. Correspondence between the Post Office, the Treasury and the Office of Public Works (OPW) culminated in a decision in October 1917 to write off almost all of the £149,744 book value of the GPO building and land given uncertainty over 'how far the walls now standing can be utilised for a new building or to what extent, if any, the value of the debris may exceed the cost of clearing the site'.[5]

Once the fires had died out and the GPO site was judged safe to examine, Board of Works architects surveyed the ruins. They were not troubled about the technicalities of accounting write-offs and, finding the shell structurally intact, drew up preliminary plans for rebuilding. By 12 August Howard Pentland had come up with a rough sketch of a possible ground plan but there was no unanimity at either the operational or political level on the wisdom of rebuilding on the existing site. The future of the GPO became a question on which everyone felt entitled to express an opinion. Those keen to emphasise the opportunities for increasing operational efficiency put the argument for moving the Post Office closer to Amiens Street railway station,

---

4. BPMA Post 31/80.
5. NAI TEC/94341/21.

where sorting and conveyance arrangements might be more efficiently integrated. Others cast their eyes around for a building that might be pressed into service immediately as a GPO, with Gandon's Custom House being mentioned as a potential candidate. Those of a political bent saw a chance to rebuild on the GPO site but create, instead of a remodelled Post Office, a parliament building that would house the legislature of the self-governing Ireland that was due to emerge under the postponed Home Rule legislation. Such was the view of one architectural authority, Mr R. Caulfield Orpen, president of the RIAI, who was a brother of the noted artist William Orpen and in 1922 was himself prepared to submit a design for the new stamps to be issued on independence. He envisaged the creation, from the ruins of Talbot and Earl Streets, of a wide new boulevard and argued:

> We have a Home Rule Bill on the Statute Book and shall be needing a House of Parliament; what could be better than to place this … where the General Post Office used to be.

He thought, a trifle optimistically perhaps, that this would appeal particularly to Ulstermen, whose:

> first view on leaving Amiens Street Station is of the House of Parliament beckoning to them from up a beautiful avenue to send their members to take their rightful share in the government of the country they love.[6]

Speculation on the future of the GPO was certainly widespread and it seems that there were divergent views not just in Dublin but also on the other side of the Irish Sea. While Board of Works architects in Dublin had decided that the GPO shell was structurally sound, it was reported that authorities in England were taking a different view. The *Irish Builder* reported that the London correspondent of one of the Irish papers had heard:

> it is the intention of the Government to demolish the shell of the General Post Office in Sackville Street, and that this decision is based on the advice of the English office of Public Works, who consider the shell does not lend itself to future development.

Finding it hard to believe that 'any such act of sheer vandalism could be contemplated' and dismissing as absurd the pretext 'that the walls do not lend themselves to future extension', *The Irish Builder* warned Dublin's citizens to be watchful and reminded them how the government's decision on the Loopline Bridge had destroyed the wonderful view of Gandon's Custom House. In relation to the destruction of the building's interior, the editor took the view that 'The complete

---

6. *The Irish Builder* (1916) vol. 58, no. 15.

gutting of the interior may be a blessing in disguise, offering a chance for replanning on better and more academic lines.'[7] The destruction wrought by the rebellion and the gradual demolition and clearing, by a large number of demobilised soldiers after the war, of the ruined buildings surrounding it certainly displayed the magnificence of the GPO façade to full advantage and provided an opportunity for considering the redevelopment of the city centre and its main thoroughfare. The widening of Prince's Street and the upper part of Henry Street, as far down as Moore Street, might have created a new civic plaza with the GPO at its centre, but this did not happen. Perhaps it was just as well, because as it turned out, there would be further destruction of the city centre within a few years and the opportunity to reflect on the rebuilding of Sackville Street would occur within the context of what was quite an ambitious piece of legislation, the Reconstruction (Emergency Provisions) Act of 1924.

The top floor of the Amiens Street Parcels Office became the Central Telegraph Office after the Rising and business was conducted here until 1932, when staff moved back to the GPO.
(© Royal Mail Group Ltd 2014, courtesy of the British Postal Museum & Archive)

7. *Ibid.*

In the immediate aftermath of the rebellion, it was the practicalities of finding new administrative and operational accommodation that occupied the attention of senior GPO staff. The temporary letter-sorting office, established in the Rotunda Rink, occupied a large steel and wooden structure that had been set up as a commercial venture within what was Rutland Square Gardens by an enterprising businessman, Frank Chambers, in 1909. On 3 May the postmaster general took over the building on the basis that it was required for the public service of the Crown. The position was regularised a year later by James MacMahon, GPO secretary, when he signed an indenture between the governors of the Rotunda Hospital and the postmaster general agreeing to pay £235 rent and carry on Post Office business in a manner that would do no injury to the health and comfort of the Rotunda's patients. As so often happens, what had been set up as emergency sorting accommodation put down roots and might still be there, indeed, but for the fact that it was destroyed by anti-Treaty troops in November 1922.

Essential telegraph work had been carried on by Post Office staff during the Rising from accommodation provided by the Great Northern Railway Company, and after the end of the rebellion this service was transferred a few yards down the street to the top floor of the Parcels Office in Amiens Street. The Central Telegraph Office continued to be based here until it moved back to a newly constructed office in the GPO on 24 April 1932, sixteen years to the day since its staff were forced out on Easter Monday 1916. The GPO's administrative staff, the secretariat, found refuge at 16 Upper Sackville Street and the building was suitably modified to allow the creation of a new public office there as well. Next door to No. 16, known as Sackville Hall, was the accounting department of the GPO. These three buildings formed, in effect, Dublin's GPO until July 1922, when they were destroyed by the fires that engulfed that side of the street at the start of the Civil War. The secretariat's staff had been moved in April 1922 to Dublin Castle and were housed in the building formerly known as La Touche's Bank.

There is no doubt that in the years from 1916 to the end of the Civil War, the GPO and its staff had suffered more than any other government department. The frequent moves and the destruction of so much of its day-to-day administrative and operational record imposed a considerable burden on its staff. There was also believed to be a degree of personal danger attached to the work of some GPO officials. In June 1922, when the Civil War began, army revolvers were distributed among the personal staffs of ministers, including in some cases the secretaries of government departments. The temporary GPO and its operations were targeted by anti-Treaty forces during the Civil War, and added to this was a very tense industrial relations climate. Many postal staff, who had seen their wages cut by the government's elimination of the cost-of-living bonus paid to all civil servants, faced severe hardship. The postmaster general, J. J. Walsh, though himself a former Post Office man, knew that the financial position of the new state was precarious, and when postal staff went on strike in September his response was very robust.

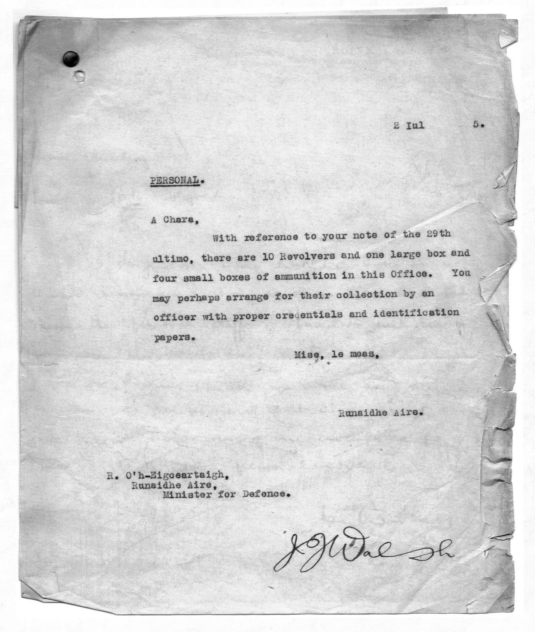

2 Iul   5.

PERSONAL.

A Chara,

     With reference to your note of the 29th
ultimo, there are 10 Revolvers and one large box and
four small boxes of ammunition in this Office.   You
may perhaps arrange for their collection by an
officer with proper credentials and identification
papers.

          Mise, le meas,

          Runaidhe Aire.

R. O'h-Eigceartaigh,
   Runaidhe Aire,
      Minister for Defence.

A note from J. J. Walsh seeking the collection of the arms which had been issued to certain GPO staff at the time of the 1922 strike.

When one member of staff, Olive Flood, was wounded by the troops who had been deployed by the government, the mood became extremely tense and there was a real risk of violence breaking out. Revolvers and ammunition were issued to some GPO officials who worked in the Dublin postal district and who were obliged to pass pickets. Each gave a receipt in the form 'Received from the postmaster general one Colt Revolver & six rounds of ammunition'. The strike resulted in defeat for the postal staff and it left, in the context of the 1913 Lockout and the involvement of organised labour in the 1916 Rising, a bitter legacy. Fortunately, however, the guns issued to GPO staff saw no official use and ten Colt revolvers, one large box and four small boxes of ammunition were returned to Dick Hegarty, private secretary to the minister for defence, on 28 February 1927. An earlier note written from an unnamed GPO official on 2 July 1925 to P. P. McMenamin in the minister's office mentions that all guns had been accounted for 'except one revolver which was subsequently recovered from a chap named Ryan who got 18 months or 2 years for holding up people'.[8] The 1922 strike was a reaction to the severe hardship facing many Post Office staff. It was also a test of the new state's authority. In the context of a decade of disruption, the capacity and willingness of staff, during these difficult years, to reorganise themselves to maintain the many services for which the GPO was responsible, is very creditable.

As the staff of the GPO gradually settled into their new premises around the city and the running of the Post Office returned to normal, attention was given once more to day-to-day matters that had been set aside as all efforts were concentrated on rebuilding the department's infrastructure after the rebellion. Organised dining facilities for staff, for instance, which were particularly important for those working at night and which had been provided in the canteen of the GPO, had been disrupted. A GPO and other departmental dining clubs needed to be reactivated in Dublin. By the autumn of 1916 plans had been formed to establish within the Parcels Office in Amiens Street what was described as a 'refreshment club' and the inaugural meeting of the GPO (Amiens Street, Dublin) Refreshment Club was duly held at the Office of the Controller Telegraphs at 6 p.m. on Thursday 26 October 1916. Its minutes provide an interesting insight into the management of a small-scale catering business a century ago and, through its menus, highlight changes in dietary habits. Table 2 (overleaf) gives an indication of what was on offer to staff.

After formal adoption of its rules, the committee appointed Mr Feeney as secretary and Mr Tutty as treasurer and accepted Mrs Lowry's (née Miss Kennedy) offer to act as cook at approximately £1 per week. They fixed the wages of the head waitresses at 17s. per week and the overtime rate for all staff at 6d. an hour with National Insurance contributions to be paid by the club. Mr Archer, Victualler, of Talbot Street, was selected as meat contractor, Hanlon's

8. An Post archives.

or McCabe's would supply fish, Messrs Roberts of Suffolk Street was chosen for coffee, and between them the principal Dublin bakeries, Johnston, Mooney & O'Brien and Kennedy's, would provide bread. There would have been no call, of course, for most alcoholic drinks in a staff dining club, but beer was important and it was decided that porter would be sought directly from Guinness. The purchase of cutlery, linen, pots, pans, stationery, books and membership cards was left in the hands of the secretary and the Munster and Leinster Bank, Sackville Street branch, was appointed to handle the club's banking arrangements. The secretary, it was agreed, would be paid £35 and, on the basis of the amount of work to be done, he certainly earned it.

Having set up the framework within which the club was to operate, the committee left consideration of matters like pricing to a later meeting. It was a wise decision, for the minutes of the November meeting record that 'A prolonged discussion took place regarding the fixing of prices for various articles.' In a city centre which had endured privation during the course of the recent destructive rebellion and where the memory of the severe hardship of the 1913 Lockout would have been very keen, the setting of prices for staff would naturally have encouraged vigorous debate among the committee members. It was unanimously decided to charge separately for potatoes at the rate of one penny per portion and to charge members 1d. for cooking their own material. A charge would not, however, be levied for boiling eggs brought in by staff. Mugs of tea would be provided so long as members brought their own mugs, and a slice of bread would be included in the price of every dinner. In the end, a detailed price list was agreed and the date of the opening of the new club was fixed for Monday 6 November 1916.

TABLE 2 —

GPO REFRESHMENT CLUB

Bacon (Irish) per rasher	2d.
Bread & Butter per slice	½d.
Coffee, ground, per cup	1½d.
Beef Corned (only) (large)	8d.
Irish Stew (small)	6d.
Fish	Market price
Ordinary vegetables per portion	1d.
Potatoes per portion	1d.
Tea per mug	1½d. (Mugs must be provided by members)
Soup per plate	2½d.
Sweets per portion	2½d. & 3½d.
Beer, stout, porter, ale & c. at ordinary prices.	

Political uncertainty and continuing unrest in Ireland meant that work on the reconstruction of the GPO did not begin until after independence and was not finally completed until 1934. An attempt was made by the new Irish government to place responsibility for the destruction of the GPO on the British government, and *Irish Life* in its issue of 17 February 1922 reported that the Irish postmaster general, J. J. Walsh, said a claim for £1,000,000 would be lodged against Britain. There was certainly a feeling within the GPO, expressed by J. J. Coonan of the Secretary's Office, that the cost of erecting a new Post Office should be discussed 'in the course of the negotiations proper to the adjustment of the financial relations between Great Britain and the Irish Free State'.[9] Walsh himself was keen that the new building should be a substantial one extending to four or possibly five storeys, but the GPO solicitor, George Reid, remembering earlier compensation payments made by the Post Office, pointed out that any significant increase in height, especially on the Henry Street side, would probably lead to a claim for infringement of ancient lights.

As the date for the establishment of the Irish Free State drew closer, it became clear that the opportunity to rebuild the GPO at the expense of the United Kingdom taxpayers had been lost. A letter from the Treasury to the Irish postmaster general made it clear that the estimates for public works for the 1922–23 financial year would be voted 'not by the Imperial Parliament, but by the new Parliament of Southern Ireland out of Irish revenues'.[10] The division of postal responsibilities between Britain and Ireland was also a subject of discussion, with the GPO in Dublin having to take over many aspects of accounting, savings-bank and money-order work that had formerly been done in London. This additional work required additional space within a reconstructed GPO, wherever it was located. While there was certainly consideration of an alternative site, the fact that the building had only just been reopened in 1916 after an extensive renovation programme meant that the design plans were still very fresh in the minds of both GPO management and Board of Works architects. When the Custom House was suggested as a possible new location, the idea was rejected by a government spokesman who stated that the GPO's 'historical and sentimental associations in connection with … Easter Week' as well as the general suitability of the location meant that the GPO would not be moving from its original site.[11] Where there was a major change in thinking was in the provision of a letter-sorting office within the GPO. In a letter of 21 February 1922 to *The Freeman's Journal*, John Ryan of Clontarf clearly expressed the case for moving the GPO to a site beside the Parcels Office in Amiens Street:

---

9. NAI TEC/b-s9484/22.
10. *Ibid.*
11. *The Freeman's Journal* (9 March 1922).

the arrangement would obviate the expense and inconvenience of fleets of vans collecting mails from four railway termini, bringing them to a congested centre in O'Connell Street, and then carting them away to the various railways.

The argument that proximity to a railway station would increase operational efficiency was a strong one and while there might have been a sentimental attachment to the idea of sorting letters in the GPO there was no reason that this should be continued. In 1916 letter sorting had moved from the GPO to the Rotunda Rink and when those premises were destroyed, the department leased space at 10 Parnell Square. The notion, consequently, that the GPO, as the administrative headquarters of the Post Office, must necessarily include a sorting office within its walls had come to be seen as false and old-fashioned and in 1923 work began on a new central sorting office adjacent to Westland Row railway station.

With the need to provide a sorting office and attendant facilities for postmen in the GPO overcome, those planning the reconstruction of the GPO were given an opportunity to think on a broader scale and to envisage a building that might incorporate something new. This, in a sense, was a bonus, because once it had been established that the original 1814–18 façade was sound, the destruction of so many neighbouring buildings presented them with a unique opportunity to develop the site. Not long after the burning embers had cooled in the GPO, minds had turned to the acquisition of property at the back of the building and expansion to the west down Henry Street. The extensive Coliseum site, which provided frontages on both Henry Street and Prince's Street, had been acquired without undue difficulty, but agreement on some of the other plots proved harder to achieve and involved some careful legal work.

Until the GPO could be rebuilt, its various departments found themselves scattered throughout the city wherever space could be found. By 1923, for instance, the newly created Irish Post Office Savings Bank was housed in a section of the old Ship Street Barracks, the engineers were in Leitrim House in Stephen Street, letter and parcel sorting took place in a number of different locations, the Central Telegraph Office was in Amiens Street, the Central Telephone Exchange in Crown Alley and headquarters functions like accounting, legal and stores operated at some distance from each other. The acquisition of extra property on the GPO site offered scope to bring some centralised order to an organisation that had been segmented by the destruction, political uncertainty and unrest of the years between 1916 and 1923.

The task of creating a new GPO building that would reunite many of these functions fell to an OPW team that contained able men like Harold Leask, W. H. Cooke, D. M. Turner and J. M. Fairweather and which was led by T. J. Byrne, principal architect of the OPW.

OPPOSITE: *J. J. Walsh, who had started his career as a Post Office clerk in Cork and was in the GPO in 1916, was appointed postmaster general after independence in 1922.*

S.B. No. 63.

banc Taisce an poist
(POST OFFICE SAVINGS BANK)

Deintean ʒnó bainc Taipce an poipt pan Oipiʒ peo. Téiʒeann an Rialtap in uppúp aip ʒo ʒcoimeádpap ʒo plán pábálta ʒac a ʒcuippean i mbanc Taipce an poipt aʒup péadpaip do cuid ainʒid mapaon le húp aip d'aiptappainʒ aon uaip a ceaptóið pé uait.

Tuʒtap amac in aipce do ʒac taipceoip leabap Taipce ina ʒcuiptean an bpeacað ʒac taipce a deintean. Ina ceannta pin deineann an Ppíom-Oipiʒ, baile áta cliat ʒac taipce de £20 nó níop mó d'admáil ʒo ppepialta.

Ip peappde tú cuntap a beit aʒat pa banc Taipce. Paiʒ aʒ an ʒcún-tap duilleoʒ ina bpuil lán-míniú ap buntáiptí an bainc.

Post Office Savings Bank business is trans-acted at this Office. The safety of your deposits in the Post Office Savings Bank is guaranteed by the Government, and the amount can be withdrawn with interest, at any time you require it.

A deposit Book, in which each deposit made is recorded, is issued free of charge to every de-positor. In addition all deposits of £20 and upwards are specially acknowledged by the Chief Office, Dublin.

It will be to your benefit to open an account. Ask at the counter for leaflet explaining ad-vantages in full.

L. Ó bROIN,
Rúnaí.

an Roinn poipt aʒup teleʒpapa.
baile áta cliat.

(B.74).P5100—1,000.5/54.A.7.&.Co.,Ltd. G.1.

Following independence, detailed discussions took place between GPO and British Post Office officials on how best to make arrangements for businesses like the Post Office Savings Bank.

T. J. Byrne led the OPW team that was responsible for the rebuilding of the GPO and other buildings in Dublin's city centre. (Courtesy of the Irish Architectural Archive)

Thomas Byrne was born in 1876 in England, son of a Carlow-born Royal Irish Fusilier and an English mother, and his earlier life was spent there. A period working for a Drogheda architect, Anthony Scott, re-established a connection with Ireland and he ended up marrying Scott's daughter. Work for London County Council was followed by his appointment in 1901 as architect to South Dublin Rural District Council, where he made use of his London experience to pioneer an improved standard of public housing in Dublin. Developments in Rathfarnham and Mount Brown are notable, as is his execution of work, in an arts and crafts style, on the Carnegie libraries in Clondalkin and Whitechurch. He was appointed principal architect of the OPW in 1923 and in that role was the lineal descendant of Francis Johnston. Each was destined to work on some of the great classical buildings of Dublin – Parliament House, the Four Courts, the Custom House and, of course, the General Post Office – and had the opportunity to appreciate the talents of those who had gone before them. Of that quartet, three had been destroyed or substantially damaged in the recent past and for Byrne there must have been, to some extent, a sense of historical as well as architectural expectation associated with his work on them. Hidden behind a somewhat reticent manner was a man who brought to his profession a keen understanding of modern materials, a purposeful focus and a meticulous attention to his task. At the time of his appointment to the OPW he was interviewed by *The Irish Builder*, which observed that people would be mistaken if they assumed 'a certain slowness of speech, and an unusual reserve' signified 'lack of interest in the matter under discussion'. Such a conclusion could not, it went on, be further from the truth:

> A false argument or a slovenly statement will at once discover to the unfortunate speaker that behind a quiet and unassuming demeanour an active mind and an exceptionally attentive memory are working, and that Mr Byrne is as shrewd in his judgement as he is strong in his determination.[12]

That determination and judgement, nurtured by his early experience of London's architectural grandeur and awareness of Dublin's social deprivation, must have helped him as he approached the job of reconstructing the principal public buildings of a proud city with a turbulent past.

---

12. *The Irish Builder* (1923) vol. 65, no. 10.

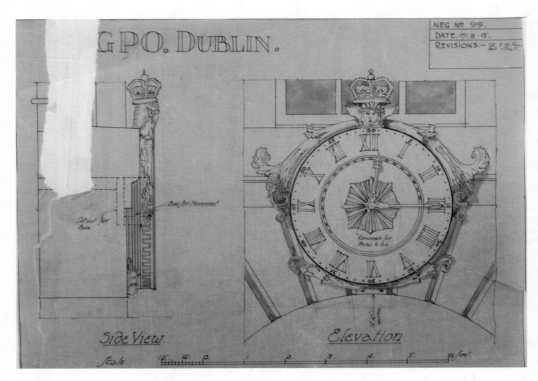

OPPOSITE AND ABOVE: *A study in chronology. The 1915 design for the clock to be placed under the GPO portico (opposite top), T. J. Byrne's drawing (opposite bottom), which dispenses with the Roman numerals and inserts the Irish harp, and the clock as it may be seen today.* (Drawings courtesy of the Office of Public Works, photograph: Author's Collection)

By separating the task of rebuilding the GPO into distinct segments, Byrne adopted the same technique as Cochrane and Pentland a couple of decades earlier. The building fell naturally into blocks – Johnston's original portico and ornamental façade and the Henry Street and Prince's Street wings, which had been developed as part of the renovation and extension work undertaken by Cochrane and Pentland. The extra property acquired after 1916 on both sides of the main block allowed Byrne to envisage much longer elevations to both Henry Street and Prince's Street and to plan connecting blocks between the two sides. What was strikingly innovative in his designs for the new GPO was the incorporation of shops into the structure at ground level on both wings and the introduction of a covered shopping arcade, much less ornate but in the style of something like the Galleries Royales Saint-Hubert in Brussels, linking Henry Street with Prince's Street.

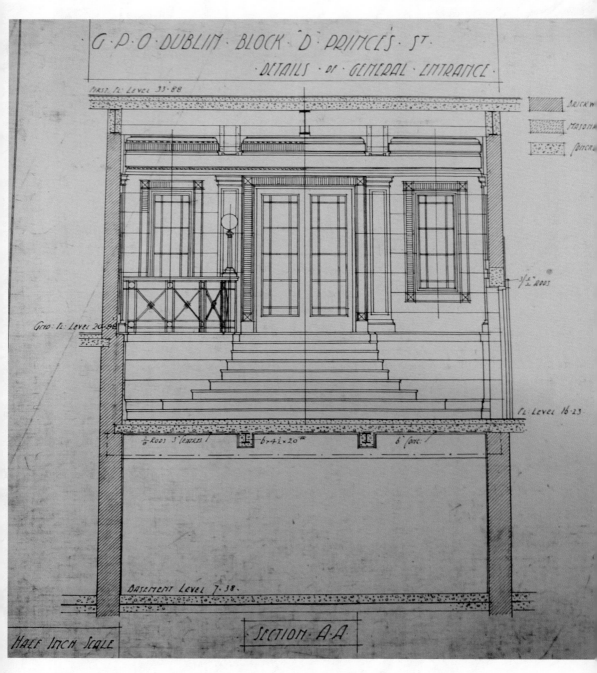

ABOVE AND OPPOSITE: *The design for the main Prince's Street entrance to the GPO envisaged a gracious staircase rising to an art deco doorway flanked by internal windows. The style is maintained in the detail of an internal door frame.* (Plan courtesy of the Office of Public Works, photograph: Author's Collection)

This was a felicitous touch, as it established a nice historical link with the College Green GPO, which after its move to Sackville Street in 1818 had been remodelled, under the name of the Royal Arcade, as Dublin's first shopping centre, comprising some thirty shops selling everything from perfumes and hosiery to toys and tobacco. It also recognised the GPO's underlying commercial potential and purpose and set it at the centre of what was arguably Dublin's prime shopping district. The Prince's Street Arcade, with some art deco touches that characterised much of the internal decoration of Byrne's GPO, was constructed under a parabolic glazed roof and finished with enriched plaster and granite pilasters, Ionic columns and entablature framing, all of which were in keeping with the classical style of the façade. The overall effect was pleasing and for many years the Arcade had a strong anchor tenant in Woolworths' shop which had its side entrance there, the main doors being on the Henry Street frontage. Some will also remember the Arcade as home of the Government Publications Office and as the first base of the GPO's philatelic shop for stamp collectors. Today, the Arcade is managed by a subsidiary company of An Post and its traders continue to offer a range of useful goods and services to those taking the short cut between the two streets.

The reconstruction of the GPO started with the Henry Street elevation and Byrne's plan for this was based on the development of thirteen shops at ground level on Henry Street with postal accommodation on the four upper floors. The retail development was handled on the basis of recruiting tenants who would be responsible for the construction of their premises in line with the OPW's plans. Demand for shops on what was then known as The Post Office Buildings site was strong and in 1925 a good start was made on the work. Tenders had also been sought for reinstatement of the GPO façade, and this job was begun on 23 August 1925. Progress on the front was initially slow because of a shortage of heavy steel girders and stanchions, and P. S. O'Hegarty, the secretary, had to explain that the anticipated opening of a new public office before Christmas 1926 had been delayed by 'the Coal Strike and general disturbed condition of Industrial England'.[13] Towards the end of 1926, however, most of the heavier sections had been supplied and fixed in place and a good deal had been achieved with floor, roof and general joinery work too. Byrne's design for the new public office of the GPO was very generous, and at 6,400 sq ft was even larger than the space that had been opened to the public just a few weeks before the Rising.

OPPOSITE: *Byrne's GPO Arcade was an innovative proposition, and while there has been some remodelling of the shop façades over the years, it remains an elegant and rather gracious addition to the GPO's architecture.* (Author's Collection)

---

13. NAI Department of Posts and Telegraphs, B&S 17879/29.

PREVIOUS PAGES: *An internal view of the work on the GPO's public office during reconstruction.* (Courtesy of the Irish Architectural Archive)

The glory of the office is its height and richly coffered ceiling, which in conscious tribute to Johnston reinstates his Greek fret motif that can also be seen in the decoration of the counter grilles. For the visitor who drops in to the GPO for the first time, the overall effect is impressive, the sense of space and style reminiscent of 'the lobby of a great Art Deco hotel'.[14] The public counter, some 126 ft long, curves sinuously around the edge of the office, providing plenty of positions for business. Sandstone for the lining of the public office was brought from Mountcharles in Donegal and a contract was made with the Kilkenny Marble Company for the supply of the Irish marble that would adorn the entrance porches and the walls of the public office to counter level.

14. Casey (2005) p. 147.

From its new studios in the GPO, music, documentaries and popular programmes such as Information Please *were broadcast by Radio Éireann. Its resident team of experts is pictured here.*

The Minister for Posts and Telegraphs requests the honour of the company of

Mr & Mrs J. Ryan

on the occasion of the formal reopening, by the President, of the General Post Office, O'Connell Street, Dublin, on Thursday, 11th July, 1929, at 12 noon.

R.S.V.P. to

The Secretary,
Department of Posts and Telegraphs,
(Room 46) Dublin Castle.

An invitation to the formal reopening of the GPO on 11 July 1929. Reconstruction continued on parts of the building until 1933.

By early 1928 some supply problems had been overcome and structural work on the front block and on the superstructure of the Henry Street elevation had been completed. A new connecting block in the GPO's central courtyard space, which like the shopping arcade behind it was an innovation of Byrne's, had been erected on a steel framework with fire-resistant floors. On the Prince's Street elevation, the old GPO wall had been taken down the previous year to within 10 ft of ground level and the ground excavated in preparation for the new foundations on which a steel framework could be laid. In August 1928 enough work had been completed on the front and Henry Street blocks of the GPO to gather together staff from their various outposts around the city and accommodate the whole of the accounts branch, the savings bank and the broadcasting studios. The inclusion of radio men and women among the GPO's staff was a new departure since staff had last been in the building and it reflected the government's decision, after much debate and some acrimony, to allocate responsibility for the management of Radio Éireann

BELOW: *People stand on the roof of the GPO and on the street outside in 1930 in honour of Sir Charles Kingsford Smith, the transatlantic aviator, and his Southern Cross aeroplane.* (National Library of Ireland)

to the Post Office. Initially known as 2RN, its international designation, Ireland's radio station moved from its cramped premises in Little Denmark Street, where the ILAC shopping centre is now, to spacious accommodation on the top two floors of the GPO's Henry Street block. It would stay at this location until the move to its current home in Donnybrook in 1973.

While work on the Prince's Street elevation was far from complete and there was still some finishing to be done elsewhere in the GPO, enough had been completed by the summer of 1929 to allow the public office and the Parcels Office to reopen for business. The ceremonial reopening of the building by the president took place at noon on Thursday 11 July 1929, the anniversary of the truce that had ended the War of Independence eight years earlier. Speaking from a specially constructed platform erected by the OPW in front of the GPO, Mr Cosgrave drew attention to the quality of the Irish materials and craftsmanship that had gone into rebuilding the Post Office: 'sandstone from Donegal and marble from Kilkenny, Cork and Connemara', with bronze and iron metal work done in Dublin and 'plastering, which gave much of the architectural effect … worked in place in the honoured manner of the city.' It was certainly a distinguished piece of work and a big improvement on the rather cramped space, a former car showroom in Middle Abbey Street, where GPO business had been transacted since December 1922.

Development on the Prince's Street block had been satisfactory, with reinforced ground- and first-floor work completed by 1930. A building-trade dispute in January 1931 led to a temporary stoppage of work, which affected progress. The main component of this block was the Central Telegraph Office, which had continued to operate from the Amiens Street Parcels Office since its temporary installation there in 1916. Byrne had designed a spacious new hall, 200 ft in length and 50 ft wide, which would contain the telegraph Instrument Room. It was floored with special material to minimise noise and top-lit from windows and ceiling lights. Colonel Ned Doyle, who spent most of his life in the army and retired as director of the signals corps, began his career in this room about 1936. When he met me in the GPO shortly before he died and we walked around the old CTO, he could still picture its layout – the Morse lines, the phonogram benches and the teleprinters – and recall the people who had taught him the vital importance of accuracy and timekeeping in telegraph work. When he left the GPO to join the army signals corps at the start of the Emergency, he brought with him one GPO practice he would later introduce into the army – the method of judging telegraph proficiency by counting completed telegraph messages per quarter hour instead of simply words per minute, an inferior system which took no account of clerical verification and traffic-clearance time.[15] In April 1932 telegraph staff were able to move back into the GPO, and secretariat staff, who would occupy the first and second floors on the Prince's Street wing, followed a few months later, in October.

---

15. An Post archives – interview with E. D. Doyle, 31 March 2009.

PREVIOUS PAGES: *Under a curved roof, the new telegraph Instrument Room on the Prince's Street side of the GPO was well lit and fitted out with noise-absorbent material.* (National Library of Ireland)

In 1933 the reconstruction of the GPO was finally completed. It had taken the best part of nine years, cost £276,000 (excluding heating and electrical service work, which was executed under the management of the Post Office's own engineering staff) and created a building with floor space amounting to some 190,000 sq ft. Its reconstruction was a considerable achievement for Byrne and the OPW. The retention of the historic façade and its harmonious reintegration into a new building, which had to cater for the very particular and technical requirements of a large and complex organisation, took an unusual combination of vision, patience and determination. The decision to incorporate commercial retail space in the GPO complex brought a vibrant bustle to the area, secured an additional revenue stream and avoided capital expenditure on ground- and basement-level building work on the Henry Street elevation. It is a measure of his dedication and capacity for work that Byrne was able, at the same time as he was working on the GPO, to concentrate also on the reconstruction of the Custom House and the Four Courts. It must have been a heavy responsibility. He died in 1939 and is buried in Glasnevin.

From Local Landmark to
National Symbol

With a message of life, it defiantly flies
From the sullen and smoke-stained walls,
And moist are most of the watchers' eyes
For a sacrifice brave it recalls;
But that soul-stirring cheer that rings out on the air
Is a shout of defiance to the foe
That tells him men are still ready to dare
For the flag on the G.P.O.

'The Flag on the G.P.O. Easter 1917', J. J. Walsh

The criticism at the time of its construction that the GPO was a bit off the beaten track was soon forgotten as the city grew and commercial interests, hotels and fashionable shops established themselves across the river. At its new location in Sackville Street there was space for the GPO itself to become part of a famous city spectacle that could draw visitors and locals alike to its doors. This was the regular departure of the mail-coaches from the GPO, and in the days before railway travel, people would gather in the evening to see them set out for distant towns throughout the land. Both mail and passengers were carried by the coaches and the sight of a coach-and-four, with its driver and armed mail guard, departing at 8 p.m. made Sackville Street the bustling centre of town. Although the Post Office was instrumental in having roads improved, with speeds of only five miles per hour and the risk of attack by robbers in the small hours of the night, travel would not have been easy for passengers. The Belfast coach left Dublin at 8 p.m. and, after following the line of the old Belfast road, arrived at 6 a.m. the next morning. Two coaches served Cork, one travelling via Naas, Kilkenny and Fermoy, and the other going by Athy, Cashel and Mitchelstown. At twenty-six hours, this was not a journey to be undertaken on a whim.

In 1821 Rowland Hill, at this stage more interested in educational than postal reform, was in Dublin with his brother en route to examine the educational methods employed at the school set up by Lovell Edgeworth at Edgeworthstown. They were keen to see the coaches leave from the GPO but were rather taken aback by the extent of the weaponry borne by the mail-coach guards. They expected each to have, as in England, a blunderbuss but 'found that he carried, in addition, a sword and pistols, while some of the coaches had two guards, and others even three'.[1] Malachi Horan, recalling in the early 1940s the stories his father had told him some seventy years before, conjures up the hustle and bustle of a similar scene as the mail-coaches arrived at the GPO at Christmas time in olden days:

> All of a minute they seen what they were waiting for – the Cork mail-coach and it pulling up at the post office door, every horse lathered with sweat. The guard lept down from the dickey and opened the door, and before you could say your name, the passengers were getting out and their friends meeting them. It was 'A Happy Christmas' here and 'A Merry Christmas' there, and parcels and hampers, or maybe a goose, thrown out of the boot on the ground for people to fall over. It was jolly – it was Christmas, ay, it was. God be with the old times![2]

On one occasion, just a few years after the Hill brothers had noticed the arms carried, an alleged insult over politics from one of the passengers to one of the waiting crowd overcame the Christmas spirit and led to a famous duel in Drumcondra on St Stephen's Day. From that *affaire d'honneur*, for which the Irish were alleged to have a particular fondness, only one of the two combatants left the designated field off the Whitworth Road.

The gradual acceptance of the building as a Dublin landmark and meeting point went hand in hand with its development as a centre of vital commercial importance. When the foundation stone of the new GPO was laid in 1814, the Post Office was an institution of considerable importance to the state and of much convenience to men of property, but its influence beyond these spheres was very limited, as most Irish people were poor and uneducated and had no concern with letters. It served the interests of a small minority and its management was in the hands of men whose

1. Hill, R. and Hill, G. B., *The Life of Sir Rowland Hill* (De la Rue, London, 1880) vol. 1, p. 161.
2. G. A. Little, *Malachi Horan Remembers* (Mercier Press, Cork, 1986), p. 101.

personal and professional interests were generally at one with those who governed Ireland at the time. As the Post Office was reinvented as a great democratic institution, serving the needs of everyone and offering fair and steady employment to all who could meet its entrance tests, so were people inclined to recognise and claim the GPO as their own. Its position as the principal building in Dublin's main thoroughfare also brought it to prominence. *The Freeman's Journal* of 19 December 1831, for example. carried a modest advertisement for the riding establishment of M. Lalouette, whose business, The Prince's Street Riding School, was to be found near the still 'New Post-Office'. Thanking his friends, the nobility and the numerous ladies he had had the honour of serving during the summer, he begged to:

> inform those ladies who wish to enjoy the pleasure of riding during the winter, so necessary to their health, that in his Riding School they are as safe from cold as if they were in a Drawing-room. There is a comfortable gallery, with a constant fire, for the accommodation of those ladies waiting for their friends, during the time they are taking their lessons.

The gallant Frenchman was even able to provide 'long skirts to put over their clothes, to save them the trouble of coming in riding habits'.[3]

The GPO illuminated for the visit of Queen Victoria and Prince Albert in 1849. (By permission of the Board of Trinity College Dublin)

The visit of the young Queen Victoria and her husband to Ireland in 1849 made the GPO the focal point for an event of national importance. As part of the celebrations at the time and as a variation on the usual displays of fireworks or gas lighting, an enterprising photographer and inventor, Leone Gluckman, decided to illuminate the front of the GPO with electric light shining from the top of Nelson's Pillar. Wires led from heavy batteries at the bottom of the Pillar to carbon-arc lighting devices and reflectors at the top. The *Illustrated London News*, through its illustration, brought Dublin's GPO to the attention of a wide public and reported that 'The front of the building displayed a large gas illumination stretching across the pillars' with 'the letters V. and R ... a harp, Crown and stars' prominently displayed.

---

3. *The Freeman's Journal and Daily Commercial Advertiser* (19 December 1831). The property used by Lalouette for his riding business would, in due course, be incorporated within an enlarged GPO.

The GPO, though already a clear landmark in Dublin, was, thanks to events like Queen Victoria's first visit to Ireland, commanding recognition on an international scale. By the middle of the nineteenth century it had established itself as a landmark Irish building, and as tourism developed, Sackville Street and its General Post Office became synonymous with Dublin in much the same way as Killarney encapsulated Ireland's wild natural beauty. Charles Lever, whose rollicking tales of Irish life for a time allowed him to rival Charles Dickens in popularity, has his characters meet 'under the piazza of the Post Office at half-past six' before they head off for a night's entertainment. With the footpath widened in recent times, the space outside the GPO is even more of a 'piazza' today than it was in Lever's time, but he could plot his novels in the knowledge that, for his readers, the GPO was an obvious place for people to meet. The building could be found as a cover illustration for sheet music or as a decoration on souvenir handkerchiefs and it came before the public again on the occasion of the laying of the foundation stone for the O'Connell Monument in 1864. Once again the *Illustrated London News* depicts the street filled to capacity, with some lucky visitors even lining the roof of the GPO itself. By the start of the twentieth century, following the Post Office's eventual relaxation of its rules on the transmission of postcards through the mail, picture postcards with views of the GPO, Nelson's Pillar and Sackville Street were very popular choices for visitors to Ireland's capital. The Rising provided an opportunity for enterprising publishers to bring out souvenir booklets of the rebellion and with these came also picture postcards of the GPO and the leaders of the insurrection. These and other items produced over the years helped to create in the public mind an unbreakable link between the GPO as a building and the event that took place there.

Carlisle Bridge, Sackville Street and the roof of the GPO filled with spectators present for the O'Connell Monument foundation-stone ceremony in 1864.

The formal reopening of the GPO in 1929, following its reconstruction, had been an occasion for some reflection on the part of the government of the day but it had not occurred at Easter time and references to 1916 and the struggle for independence had been muted. The position was quite different, however, six years later when Oliver Sheppard's Cuchulain statue was unveiled by President of the Executive Council of the Irish Free State Éamon de Valera in the GPO, on Easter Sunday 1935 as a memorial to the declaration of a republic in 1916. Planning for the event was meticulous and the spectacle was, despite a damp day, very impressive. The streets around the GPO had been cordoned off early in the day, the Parcels Office had been set aside as the reception room for the arriving dignitaries and an enclosure area was designated for guests not quite important enough to form part of the platform party. Mr Blake of the GPO, who had sat on the government's planning committee, had made arrangements for the provision of direct communication lines between the GPO and telephone boxes on Eden Quay and College Green. When the president arrived, he was greeted by 'sixteen men of the gallant garrison which held the G.P.O. for six memorable days … armed with the old Mauser rifles landed at Howth in 1914' and escorted into the building. Speaking in the public office of the GPO, de Valera referred to the building as 'the scene of an event which will ever be counted an epoch in our history' and added, according to a report in *The Irish Times*, that it was indeed 'a reproach … that the spot had been so long unmarked'. *The Irish Press* gave the president's address generous space, noting in particular the way he spoke of those who had signed the Proclamation:

> as he named its signatories the manner in which he named them, proudly, affectionately, almost caressingly, [he] gave all who listened in that crowded hall the measure of the nation's reverence for these immortal men.

He strove to emphasise, addressing his words more, perhaps, to the unspoken hopes of southern unionists than to the implacable hostility of Orangemen north of the border, the defining inevitability of the insurrection:

> The work of Easter Week can never be undone. Even those who do not feel any yearning for Independence themselves must realise there can never be a turning back. Before 1916, Ireland might have been content for a time with something less than Independence. After 1916, that is impossible.

His speech over, the president moved forward to unveil, at last, a memorial to the event so vividly remembered by those who listened, only to be halted by a word from one of his ministers – it was still a couple of minutes too soon, for the unveiling had been planned for noon, the very hour at which Pearse had read the Proclamation and announced the birth of the new republic.

OPPOSITE: *Cast in Brussels, Oliver Sheppard's statue of Cuchulain predates the 1916 Rising but its portrayal of youthful courage and sacrifice struck a chord with those seeking a suitable monument to the event. It was placed in the GPO in 1935.*

The intervening minutes passed awkwardly but then it was time and Sheppard's Cuchulain, thenceforth to be indissolubly linked with the GPO in 1916, was revealed as the epitome of heroic struggle against a mighty foe. The *feu de joie* rang out from the soldiers on the roof of the GPO and was followed by the booming of the field guns on O'Connell Bridge. In front of the Post Office marched the veterans of 1916, ordered according to their original garrisons, with the surviving GPO men, led by Diarmuid Lynch out in front. The soldiers of contemporary Ireland followed the warriors of the previous generation while overhead flew the military aeroplanes of the Free State.

Yet, behind these choreographed and impressive scenes, which brought forth genuine emotion and enthusiasm from those who looked on from good vantage points, there was disquiet, for this ceremony had been boycotted by several men whose presence at the GPO should have been expected. General Richard Mulcahy, veteran of the successful Ashbourne engagement of 1916 and, as a former Post Office employee knew the GPO better than most, was not there. Gearóid O'Sullivan TD was not there. W. T. Cosgrave was not there. Cosgrave, quoted in the *Irish Press* of 18 April, had said that he would not be attending because:

> The time is not yet ripe for an adequate commemoration of 1916 which would be accompanied by that generous enthusiasm indispensable to success.

The opposition Dáil parties felt the planning of the event at the GPO had been hijacked by Fianna Fáil. Mulcahy, for instance, raised one point in the Dáil when he asked the minister for defence if he was aware:

> that the only paper in which advertisements were published was the Fianna Fáil Party organ, and that no advertisements were issued to the *Irish Independent, Cork Examiner* or *Irish Times* …?

Dr Ryan, minister for agriculture who was covering for Frank Aiken, the minister for defence, could only offer the feeble response that the organising committee had had 'to pay for its own expenses and advertisements'.[4] There were questions too about the composition of the firing party on the commemoration day. A memorandum from the President's Department written on 9 April 1935 points out that:

---

4.   Dáil debates, 11 April 1935, An Post archives.

The suggestion has been made that the personnel of the firing party has been taken exclusively from men who took part on one side in the Civil War.[5]

One short letter succinctly highlights that behind the spectacle and oratory at the GPO that Easter day, political tensions were high and a legacy of bitterness divided people at an event that was supposed to symbolise renewal and unity. The curt reply of Senator Oliver St John Gogarty to President de Valera's invitation to attend the unveiling at the GPO and the Shakespearian allusions make plain the anger and contempt he feels:

> I must refuse to assist you in playing Hamlet when your Republicans are howling for Macbeth. In view of my experience of them, I consider your invitation to me personally an impertinence.[6]

Considering he had been lucky to escape execution by the anti-Treaty party during the Civil War and that his house at Renvyle in Connemara had been burned down by them, he had good reason to spurn de Valera and Fianna Fáil and decline to take part in the ceremonies at the GPO.

The importance of the GPO as a building bearing potent emotional and mythological resonance had been quickly established in the years following the Rising but the wider Post Office, administered from the GPO, also played a vital part in the creation of an identity for the new state. Postage stamps and letter boxes were drafted into service as visible icons of the new order. British stamps of King George were overprinted in Irish in 1922 and letter boxes were painted green.[7] The removal of the royal crest from the pediment of the GPO was an obvious symbolic step in forging an independent identity, and the action was mirrored by the removal of similar insignia from post offices and letter boxes throughout the country and the design of new Irish typography and logos for the widespread GPO infrastructure of pillar boxes, vans, carts and uniforms.[8] In practice, the degree to which old post boxes were modified or replaced

---

5.   NAI Taoisc/S6405.

6.   NAI Taoisc/S6405/C.

7.   The King's permission for this potential slight had, it must be said, been duly sought and the fact that he was an ardent stamp collector may have helped to smooth the path.

8.   The use of iconography in helping to establish an Irish identity is examined in *The Irish Post Box: Silent Servant and Symbol of the State*.

Sir Bertram Mackennal's beautifully engraved high-value stamps were among the normal British stamps overprinted in Irish for immediate use upon independence in 1922.

depended on normal operational requirements, and with money tight most postmasters adopted a pragmatic approach to corporate identity.

GPO officials, more than most civil servants, were also aware of the need to maintain good relations with their counterparts in London and Northern Ireland. The Post Office was part of a global system, governed by international treaties, and working contact was close with the United Kingdom in particular. The government's department of external affairs had directed in 1949 that preference in official correspondence should be given to the term Ireland as the name of the state, but in a minute to Michael Hilliard, the minister for posts and telegraphs, of 22 May 1964, Liam Ó Réagáin, who would later be appointed secretary in the GPO, admitted that the word Éire had 'slipped into some contexts … in an effort to distinguish between this State and the north-eastern portion of the country'. He emphasised that the distinction was 'of more daily concern to us than to most Departments because of the close links between communications and remittance services in the two areas'.[9] While it was government policy to refer to the 'six counties', nomenclature that some north of the border would have found disagreeable, Ó Réagáin explained that his department also used the more acceptable Northern Ireland designation in official documents and publications.

It was in this sometimes delicate milieu that officials of the GPO worked and they would naturally have followed plans to commemorate the fiftieth anniversary of the Rising with close attention. In the event, the occasion was marked by less controversy than previously and with a solemnity and broad measure of consensus that had been absent from earlier show events. The GPO was again the centrepiece of celebration, and early in 1966 an opportunity arose to achieve

---

9.　An Post archives.

something symbolic that would unite people at home and win political credit abroad. Seán Lemass, writing to Frank Aiken in January of that year, mentioned that the president had heard that the flag that flew over the GPO in 1916, which it had been believed had been among the rebellion relics personally held by King George V, was actually in the Imperial War Museum in London and was wondering if it could be retrieved before the anniversary. Enquiries were made through the Irish ambassador, John Molloy, and followed up via Sir Saville Garner of the British Commonwealth Relations Office, who contacted the museum. The outcome was that word went back to Dublin that a request for the return of the flag to Ireland would be favourably received by the trustees of the museum. Lemass wrote to the British Prime Minister, Harold Wilson, and an official handing-over ceremony was arranged for 30 March 1966, the day before the British general election. The significance of the timing was noted by the Irish civil servants making the arrangements. At the last minute, however, the carefully planned preparations were thrown into confusion when it emerged that what the Imperial War Museum was preparing to give to the

Though not yet reopened, the GPO remained an obvious place to meet, as evidenced by this cycle club assembling outside the boarded-up GPO prior to a day out. (Courtesy of Davison & Associates)

Irish ambassador was not the green Irish Republic flag that had flown over the GPO but an Irish tricolour that it had formerly displayed in the museum as the authentic 1916 GPO flag. The exhibition case had carried the following explanatory note:

On the 29th April, 1916, it was hauled down when the rebel headquarters were forced to surrender to the 3rd battalion, the Royal Irish Regiment. R. L. Owens, Lieutenant Col. Commanding 3rd Battalion, Royal Irish Regiment.

There had, of course, been two Irish flags flying from opposite corners of the GPO during the rebellion, the green Irish Republic flag with its white lettering, which had been made in Countess Markievicz's house in Leinster Road in Dublin and was hoisted aloft by Éamonn Bulfin on the Prince's Street flagpole, and the Irish tricolour that had flown from the Henry Street corner of the GPO. The difficulty was that the National Museum in Dublin already had the charred remains of the Tricolour in its collection!

PREVIOUS PAGES: *With their caps set at a suitably rakish angle, these four telegram delivery boys feel infinitely superior to their comrades who have not yet graduated to motor bikes.*

What had started out as a wonderful opportunity for political capital to be won by politicians on both sides of the Irish Sea and an occasion for genuine rapprochement between the Irish and British governments was threatening to become at least an embarrassing incident if not worse. Hurried research by archival staff generated a flurry of telex messages between Dublin and London, which established that the Imperial War Museum's Tricolour had actually been seized from a house in Limerick during the War of Independence and had no connection with the GPO at all. At the same time, the GPO's Irish Republic flag, which had indeed been captured by the Royal Irish Regiment but had not, at least in the recent past, been correctly displayed was found safely stored somewhere in the museum. Sir Saville Garner, to be on the safe side, duly turned up at the handing-over ceremony with both flags and told the Irish ambassador that, while he couldn't hand them both over, he was welcome to choose whichever he wanted! Molloy happily selected the green Irish Republic flag, which was brought back to Dublin and given into the

A less familiar aspect of the GPO, the utilitarian side that lies behind Johnston's classical façade. (Author's Collection)

care of the National Museum. The British government's press release, which had identified the wrong flag, was suitably altered and a somewhat delicate political situation adroitly handled to the credit of all involved. Lemass wrote to Wilson on 7 April 1966 thanking him for 'the manner, the speed and the generosity' with which his government had responded to the request for the return of the flag. The event, he went on, could 'be welcomed as yet another step towards the building of good-will … between our two countries'.[10] Harold Wilson swept to election victory.

Wilson's great rival, Edward Heath, was the catalyst for an attempted occupation of the GPO a few years later. On Monday, 17 September 1973, Heath was due in Dublin for official discussions with the Taoiseach. When the Henry Street door was opened at nine o'clock, some thirty young men claiming to represent a republican group rushed the hall. The patrolman on duty at that entrance, which was the RTÉ door, had his keys forcibly taken from him and chairs and tables were piled up on the stairs as a barricade. Jack Storrs, a member of the GPO staff, was there at the time and subsequently gave a statement to the gardaí in Store Street:

> On the 17.9.1973 at about 9 am I went from my office to the end of the corridor on the second floor (Princes St.) I was unable to get through as the door was barricaded with two large presses … I looked down on the R.T.E. hallway and saw that the door leading to Henry Street was also barricaded with chairs and tables.[11]

The damage to the furniture he estimated at £23, a more modest bill than the £600,000 the government in 1922 provided in their estimates for rebuilding the GPO after the previous incursion. Following trials, twelve men were charged in the Special Criminal Court with forcible entry and occupation and malicious damage. They declined to recognise the court, but a spokesman said that the aim of the peaceful protest was to show that not all Irishmen agreed with 'the Quisling Free State Government in inviting that man [Mr Heath] here'. They went to jail.

A curiosity of the GPO's long history is the fact that until relatively recently it paid ground rents to various landlords and this, from time to time, provoked a little controversy. Deputy Thomas O'Hara raised the matter in the Dáil in March 1966 shortly before the fiftieth anniversary of the Rising and it came up again in the course of a question from Michael Keating in 1979. When it emerged in 1986 that rents due on leases dating back to the eighteenth century were still being paid to foreign landlords in England and America, the *Evening Herald* captioned its article 'Rent scandal of famous city sites'. Although the amounts being paid were tiny and the OPW maintained that the administrative cost of buying out the ground rents would be more than the rent, steps were duly taken to safeguard the integrity and honour of the nation's most famous building.

---

10. NAI Taoisc/97/6/532.

11. An Post archives.

The extraordinary range of responsibilities – from textile inspection to issuing dog licences – undertaken by the Post Office led in the 1970s to government plans for the break-up of the Department of Posts and Telegraphs into two new state companies, one for telecommunications and the other for postal and agency services. It was felt that a new organisational structure would facilitate investment and modernisation, particularly in the capital-intensive area of telecommunications. Technical and engineering staff were assigned to Telecom Éireann, the new telecommunications company, while postal staff were assigned to An Post, which continued to have its headquarters in the GPO.

The separation of responsibilities that had been shouldered for so long by a single organisation housed in a unified headquarters was not an easy task. Within the GPO it was particularly hard for those men and women who had had experience of both postal and telecommunications work during the course of their careers; the division of the old Post Office felt like the sundering of something that was fundamentally a unit, in many senses a family. For a time, those assigned to the two new organisations continued to share the GPO. It took time to relocate technical equipment, separate administrative and personal records and correctly apportion common costs between the two sides of a business that had been joined for over a century. Farewells had been said before, when some staff departed after independence in 1922 and, more recently, when the broadcasting staff moved out of the GPO. Those departures, however, were much less significant in scale and, in truth, the radio and broadcasting branch, while operating within the Department of Posts and Telegraphs, had always been seen as a distinct unit.

The departure of certain sections and staff from the GPO led to some internal remodelling of the building and in 1990 cleaning and repair work was carried out on the stonework at roof level, where there was erosion to the cornice and balustrade and there lingered the consequences of the demolition of Nelson's Pillar by the army in 1966. John Smyth's statues had also suffered serious damage from pollution over the years and were removed, with casts erected in their place. Within the last few years the public office has been repainted and its fittings renovated but there has been no structural alteration undertaken.

The suggestion that the Abbey Theatre might find a new home within the GPO as part of a grand retail development received, in the eyes of those who worked in the building at least, rather more serious consideration than it deserved, but the project, fortunately, came to nothing as the country came to terms with the reality of economic mismanagement. It must be added that the idea of creating a public amphitheatre of some description within the GPO was not entirely new. When the building stood as a mere shell in 1922, one correspondent of *The Freeman's*

The stump of Nelson's Pillar after it was blown up by republicans, though not, apparently,
the IRA according to the press placard. (Courtesy of the National Library of Ireland)

Journal had proposed that it be rebuilt not as a GPO but as municipal offices 'with a very badly
wanted great public hall as its central feature'.[12]

---

12. *The Freeman's Journal* (21 February 1922).

PREVIOUS PAGES: *The GPO's public office is a space of light-filled grandeur as well as the principal business centre of An Post.*

Today the GPO's public office certainly serves as an inviting space for visitors as well as customers. School children and tour groups drop in to admire its beauty and reflect on its history, and the tradition of a nativity scene and carols at Christmas time has wide appeal. A small postal museum and exhibition, *Letters, Lives & Liberty*, located just off the main office, where a bank of telephone kiosks formerly stood, explores the influence of the Post Office and the historical significance of the GPO in Irish life. Visitors can study an original 1916 Proclamation, on display just a few yards from where it was first publicly read out, and imagine for themselves events in the GPO nearly a century ago. As the centenary of the Rising approaches, An Post hopes that its

ABOVE AND OPPOSITE: *Within an area formerly occupied by public telephones, An Post created a small museum which explores the GPO's role in communications, design and in the 1916 Rising.*

PHILIP
TREACY

Éire
82ᶜ

PHILIP
TREACY

Éire
82ᶜ

Fashion and Philately at the GPO

An Post**Museum**

display here can be expanded as part of an enlarged GPO exhibition space that will open up new perspectives on aspects of Irish history, society and life that will appeal to all who pass through the doors of the GPO.

After 200 years on O'Connell Street, the GPO has witnessed riots and rebellion and seen romance and renovation within its scarred but sturdy walls. Heroes and villains, saints and sinners daily walk beneath its chaste and noble portico but it represents above all the triumph of everyday service in the little things of life – letters and pensions and savings and bills – the things that make up the ordinary business of life and allow space for the extraordinary to happen. As it looks back over two hundred years, at the people it has known and the events it has witnessed, the grand old lady of O'Connell Street – Dublin's GPO – deserves to have its story told.

After 200 years as an impartial witness to events great and small, the GPO deserves a little fanfare of appreciation.

Bibliography

❧ ❧

PRIMARY SOURCES

An Post (AP)

British Postal Museum & Archive (BPMA)

Irish Architectural Archive (IAA)

Military Archives (MA)

National Archives of Ireland (NAI)

National Library of Ireland (NLI)

Office of Public Works (OPW)

Trinity College Dublin (TCD) Library

OFFICIAL PUBLICATIONS

HMSO: *Reports of the Postmaster General of the Post Office* (London, 1855 onwards)

House of Commons: *An Account of the Establishment of the General Post Office, in Ireland* (17 April 1822)

House of Commons: *First and Second Reports from the Select Committee on Postage* (London, 1838)

House of Commons: *Nineteenth Report of the Commissioners of Inquiry into the Collection and Management of the Revenue arising in Ireland and Great Britain – Post-Office Revenue* (London, 1829)

House of Commons: *The Ninth Report of the Commissioners appointed to Enquire into the Fees, Gratuities, Perquisites, and Emoluments, which are or have been lately received in certain Public Offices in Ireland – General Post-Office* (London, 1810)

House of Commons: *Returns Relating to the General Post-Office, Dublin* (6 April 1826)

BOOKS, ARTICLES AND THESES

1916 Rebellion Handbook (The Mourne River Press, Dublin, 1998, reprint)

Bayley-Butler, B., 'John and Edward Lees', *Dublin Historical Record*, Vol. XIII Nos. 3 & 4 (Dublin, 1953)

Betjeman, J., 'Francis Johnston, Irish Architect', *The Pavilion* (London, 1946)

Bolger, W. and Share, B., *And Nelson on his Pillar* (Nonpareil, Dublin, 1966)

Bonar Law, A. and C., *The Prints and Maps of Dublin* (The Neptune, Dublin, 2005)

Bouch, J. J., 'The Republican Proclamation of Easter Monday, 1916', *Publications of the Bibliographical Society of Ireland*, Vol. V (Dublin, 1936)

Brennan-Whitmore, W. J., *Dublin Burning – The Easter Rising from behind the Barricades* (Gill & Macmillan, Dublin, 1996)

Brewer, J. N., *The Beauties of Ireland* (Sherwood, Jones, London, 1825)

Building for Government – OPW 1900–2000 (Office of Public Works, Dublin, 1999)

Byrne, J. and Fewer, M., *Thomas Joseph Byrne: Nation Builder* (South Dublin County Council, Dublin, 2013)

Carr, J., *The Stranger in Ireland* (Richard Philips, London, 1806)

Casey, C., *Dublin* (Yale University Press, New Haven, 2005)

Catterson-Smith, E., 'What Dublin owes to Francis Johnston' in *The Lady of the House* (Wilson Hartnell, Dublin, 1902)

Caulfield, M., *The Easter Rebellion* (Gill & Macmillan, Dublin, 1995)

Clarke, P., *Dublin Calling* (Radio Telefís Éireann, Dublin, 1986)

Craig, M., *Dublin 1660–1860* (Cresset Press, London, 1952)

Craig, M., *The Architecture of Ireland* (Batsford, London, 1982)

Crowe, C. (ed.), *Guide to the Military Service (1916–1923) Pensions Collection* (Óglaigh na hÉireann, Dublin, 2012)

Cuimhneachán 1916: A Commemorative Exhibition of the Irish Rebellion 1916 (National Gallery of Ireland, Dublin, 1966)

Curtis, J., *Times, Chimes and Charms of Dublin* (Verge Books, Dublin, 1992)

Daunton, M. J., *Royal Mail: The Post Office since 1840* (Athlone Press, London, 1985)

De Paor, L., *On the Easter Proclamation and Other Declarations* (Four Courts Press, Dublin, 1997)

Devine, F., *Connecting Communities* (Communications Workers' Union, Dublin, 2013)

Dittmann, M., *The Dublin Penny Post* (FAI, Wemding, 1992)

Dublin Delineated in Twenty-six Views of the Principal Public Buildings (W. F. Wakeman, Dublin, 1834)

Feldman, D. and Kane, W., *Handbook of Irish Postal History* (D. Feldman Ltd., Dublin, 1975)

Feldman, D., *Handbook of Irish Philately* (D. Feldman Ltd., Dublin, 1968)

Ferguson, P., *The A to Z of Georgian Dublin* (Harry Margary, Kent, 1998)

Ferguson, S., *The Irish Post Box: Silent Servant and Symbol of the State* (An Post/Associated Editions, Dublin, 2009)

Ferguson, S., *Business as Usual: GPO Staff in 1916* (Mercier Press, Cork, 2012)

Fisher, D., *Broadcasting in Ireland* (Routledge & Kegan Paul, London, 1978)

FitzGerald, D., *Desmond's Rising: Memoirs 1913 to Easter 1916* (Liberties Press, Dublin, 2006)

Fitzpatrick, S. A. O., *Dublin: A Historical and Topographical Account of the City* (Methuen, London, 1907)

Fox, R. M., *The History of the Irish Citizen Army* (James Duffy & Co., Dublin, 1944)

Freeman's Journal, The

Gilbert, J. T., *A History of the City of Dublin* (McGlashan and Gill, Dublin, 1859)

Gorham, M., *Forty Years of Irish Broadcasting* (Talbot Press, Dublin, 1967)

Hall, F. G., *The Bank of Ireland 1783–1946* (Hodges Figgis, Dublin, 1949)

Hamilton, E., *Dublin Doggerels* (Smyth, Dublin, 1877)

Henchy, P., 'Francis Johnston, Architect, 1760–1829' in *Dublin Historical Record*, Vol. XI, No. 1 (Dublin, 1949)

Henry, Fr, OFM Cap. (ed.), *The Capuchin Annual* (Dublin, 1966)

Hill, J., *Irish Public Sculpture* (Four Courts Press, Dublin, 1988)

Hill, R. and Hill, G. B., *The Life of Sir Rowland Hill* (De la Rue, London, 1880)

Illustrated London News, The

Irish Builder, The

Irish Times, The

Irwin, W., *Betrayal in Ireland* (The Northern Whig, Belfast [n.d.])

Jeffery, K., *The GPO and the Easter Rising* (Irish Academic Press, Dublin, 1999)

Joyce, H., *The History of the Post Office* (Bentley, London, 1893)

Leet, A., *A Directory to the Market Towns, Villages, Gentlemen's Seats and Other Noted Places in Ireland* (Brett Smith, Dublin, 1814)

Little, G. A., *Malachi Horan Remembers* (Mercier Press, Cork, 1986)

Lynch, D., *The IRB and the 1916 Rising* (Mercier Press, Cork, 1957)

Madden, D. and Louis, K., *The Dublin Find: The Most Important Stamp Find in GB Philately* (Mike Jackson, Melton Mowbray, 2006)

McCullough, N., *Dublin: An Urban History* (Anne Street Press, Dublin, 1989)

McGregor, J. J., *New Picture of Dublin* (Archer, Dublin, 1821)

McParland, E., 'Francis Johnston, Architect, 1760–1829' in *Quarterly Bulletin of the Irish Georgian Society*, Vol. XII, Nos. 3 & 4 (Dublin, 1969)

Muir, D. N., *Postal Reform and the Penny Black: A New Appreciation* (National Postal Museum, London, 1990)

Mulcahy, R., *Richard Mulcahy (1866–1971): A Family Memoir* (Aurelian Press, Dublin, 1999)

Nelson's Pillar: A Description of the Pillar with a List of the Subscribers (Chambers, Dublin, 1846)

New Picture of Dublin (William Curry, Dublin, 1835)

Norway, Mrs H., *The Sinn Féin Rebellion As I Saw It* (Smith, Elder & Co., London, 1916)

O'Brien, J. and Guinness, D., *Dublin: A Grand Tour* (Weidenfeld & Nicolson, London, 1994)

Ó Broin, L., *Just Like Yesterday* (O'Brien Press, Dublin)

O'Neill, P. C., *A Brief Review of the Irish Post Office 1784–1831* (1831, [Dublin, 1831])

Osborough, W. N., *Law and the Emergence of Modern Dublin* (Irish Academic Press/ILHS, Dublin, 1996)

Osley, J., *Built for Service: Post Office Architecture* (BPMA, London, 2010)

Pearson, P., *The Heart of Dublin* (O'Brien Press, Dublin, 2000)

Peter, A., *Dublin Fragments: Social and Historic* (Hodges Figgis, Dublin, 1928)

Pückler-Muskau, H., *Tour in England, Ireland, and France in the years 1828 and 1829* (Effingham Wilson, London, 1832)

Record of the Irish Rebellion of 1916 (*Irish Life*, Dublin, 1916)

Reynolds, M., *A History of the Irish Post Office* (MacDonnell White, Dublin, 1983)

Robinson, H., *The British Post Office* (Princeton University Press, New Jersey, 1948)

Shaw, H., *The Dublin Pictorial Guide & Directory* (Friar's Bush Press, Belfast, 1988, reprint of 1850 ed.)

Smith, G. R., *Half-a-Century in the Dead Letter Office* (W. C. Hemmons, Bristol, 1908)

St. Martin's-Le-Grand (London, 1890–1933)

Stephens, J., *The Insurrection in Dublin* (Maunsel, Dublin 1916)

Super, R. H., *Trollope in the Post Office* (Ann Arbor, Michigan, 1981)

Trevelyan, G. M., *An Autobiography & Other Essays* (Longmans, Green & Co., London, 1949)

Trollope, A., *An Autobiography* (Oxford University Press, Oxford, 1923)

Wall, T. F., *Some Notes Towards a History of Telecommunications with Particular Reference to Ireland* (Unpublished, 1997)

Walsh, J. J., *Recollections of a Rebel* (The Kerryman Ltd, Tralee, 1944)

Warburton, J., Whitelaw, J. and Walsh, R., *History of the City of Dublin* (Cadell & Davies, London, 1818)

Whittock, N., *A Picturesque Guide through Dublin* (Cornish, London, [1846])

Wilson, W., *The Post-Chaise Companion or Travellers Directory through Ireland* (Dublin, 1786)

Wright, G. N., *An Historical Guide to the City of Dublin* (Four Courts Press/Irish Academic Press, Dublin, 1980, reprint of 1825 ed.)

Index